HUMOUR AMONG THE LAWYERS

HUMOUR
AMONG THE LAWYERS

BY
JOHN AYE

LONDON
THE UNIVERSAL PRESS
CHICHESTER HOUSE, CHANCERY LANE, W.C.2

First Published . . . October 1931

Made and Printed in Great Britain by
Hazell, Watson & Viney, Ltd., London and Aylesbury.

PREFACE

By Ian Hay

ANECDOTES are the small change of History, but let us not despise them on that account. The three-penny bit is held in no great esteem (outside Scotland), but make a heap of threepenny bits and you have a bank balance.

Similarly, an anthology of personal observations and first-hand experiences in a particular sphere —Parliament, the Theatre, the Services, and the like—judiciously selected and blended, assumes the collective importance of a family archive.

That is why I welcome these volumes, more especially since their ingredients have been drawn from such authentic and readable sources. You may tackle them in two ways: either you may swallow them whole for instruction or peck at them delicately for entertainment; but in either case your reputation as a *raconteur* will be materially increased.

CONTENTS

INTRODUCTION

By J. A. R. Cairns

THE dock is a place where men and women are driven back to the stark realism of things.

Like life itself, it is packed with paradoxes, incongruities, absurdities; laughter jostles the heels of despair, sunshine peeps through clouds and shadows, yet everything seems just as it ought to be.

A jester on the Bench would be an atrocity—so would an undertaker's mute.

It is the thrill and throb of human emotions, actions and reactions that keep the Law from the acid unreality of Logic and Metaphysics. The Schoolmen live with cobwebs.

This book confessedly deals with the lighter, brighter hours of the Law.

A Book of Sorrows could be written, for the Criminal Court is the most sorrowful place on earth.

This is not such a book—rather it presents those gay interludes that lighten just a little the grim and pitiful world where many of us labour.

That it will fulfil one purpose I am certain: the reader will discover that criminals have a queer resemblance to him and me—and the bishop.

I

LAWYERS IN GENERAL

It is doubtful if the Law has ever been better described than it was by George Bernard Shaw, when he said that we look for too much from it. "We expect it," he continued, "to be ideal and almost inspired, whereas it is only an imperfect rough-and-ready device of mankind to keep people from sending each other to the devil." As a general rule we are prone to forget that it is a two-edged weapon, protective as well as despotic, and in the hardships of the latter we lose sight of the benefits of the former.

Its despotic side has been wonderfully portrayed by Mr. J. A. R. Cairns, in his book, *The Loom of the Law*. "This, then," he writes, "is the loom of the Law, and its threads are human souls. Into the texture of its weavings are woven threads of many colours, white and gold, black and crimson and grey. It is a fabric of joy and sorrow, of laughter and tears, and across it breaks at times the sunshine of children's faces and sometimes the shadows of women's broken hearts. The loom has been built piece by piece throughout long genera-

tions. It is a vast complex machine of infinite
parts, and it bears the impress of manifold limita-
tions. It is called upon to do dreadful things.
In the sorting of its threads it probes into the
deepest depths of the human soul. It dissects the
emotions, it lays bare the human heart and cuts it
bit by bit. It weaves the thread of love and hate,
of lust and greed, and its beams are often stained
with the crimson of human blood. The loom kills
men, and it breaks the hearts of women and makes
orphans of unborn children. Every living soul is
within the reach of its machinery, and you and I
may be of its weaving to-morrow. Men are struck
dumb with dismay, and women blind with grief.
As we watch it day by day the problems of life
grow into a vast, blinding, bewildering perplexity.
Who knows his destiny? A frailty, a hidden vice,
a secret sin, the weakness of a moment:

" Then comes the mist and the blinding rain
   And life is never the same again! "

The general opinion of the layman on lawyers is
well expressed by the epitaph, written by Ben
Jonson, on a local Surrey lawyer, who, contrary
to the practice of his kind, had done his best to
keep people from going to law. It runs as follows:

> " God works wonders now and then,
> Here lies a lawyer, an honest man."

A stranger, passing through the churchyard, who noticed this inscription, is reputed to have exclaimed, " What! Two of them buried in the same grave? "

No less scathing was the celebrated Lord Brougham, who once ironically defined a lawyer as " a learned gentleman who rescues your estate from your enemies and keeps it to himself." Sweeping as this is, it perhaps does not so well express public opinion as did the prisoner who was asked if he was defended by counsel, and replied, " No, my lord, I'm going to tell the truth."

There are few poets or writers who have not had a jibe at the Law, not the least well known of which is Tom Moore's epitaph on an attorney:

> " Here lies John Shaw,
> Attorney-at-Law,
> And when he died
> The devil cried,
> ' Give me your paw,
> John Shaw,
> Attorney-at-Law.' "

Somewhat similar is Hood's well-known verse:

" He saw a lawyer killing a viper
On a dunghill beside his own stable;
And the devil smiled, for it put him in mind
Of Cain and his brother Abel."

Finally, there is the remark, made by Dr. Johnson to a numerous company concerning a gentleman who had just quitted the room. " I don't care to speak ill of any man behind his back, but I believe the person who has just taken his departure is an attorney."

It remained for an Irish court crier, however, to endow the profession with a new quality, when he called out on one occasion, " All ye blackguards that isn't lawyers must leave the court."

That lawyers have always been creators of strife is almost a universal opinion. This is emphasised by an epitaph in Richmond Church to a certain Robert Lawes, Esq., who, though a barrister, " was so great a lover of peace that when a contention arose between Life and Death, he immediately yielded up the ghost to end the dispute."

In view of the opinions currently held of the legal profession, it is easy to accept the common idea that no lawyer ever goes to Heaven, but, as a matter of fact, there is, as usual, the exception to prove the rule. It is said that a solicitor who had been refused entrance to Heaven by St. Peter because he was a lawyer contrived to throw his hat inside the door, and being permitted by the kindly saint to go in and fetch it, took advantage of the fact that St. Peter, as doorkeeper, was unable to leave his post, and refused to come out again.

Less successful in times past were the attempts of lawyers to get into the House of Commons, and there are many Acts of Parliament and Ordinances disqualifying them from so doing. Prynne, the Puritan zealot, was very strong on their exclusion, which, with a knowledge of their prolixity, he declared would " shorten the duration of the session, facilitate the despatch of business, and have the desirable effect of restoring the existing laws to their primitive Saxon simplicity and making them more like God's commandments." Something of the same idea, perhaps more crudely expressed, must have been in the mind of the Czar, Peter the Great, who, while on a visit to England, remarked the crowd around the Great Hall at Westminster, and asked who they were. He was told " Lawyers." " Lawyers," said the monarch; " why, I have but two of them in the whole of my dominions, and I purpose to hang one of them the moment I get home."

Few indeed of the general public, or indeed of
the legal fraternity, know that the Law has its
patron saint. About A.D. 1300 there lived in Brit-
tany a famous lawyer, Evona or Ives, whose one
great regret in life was that his profession had no
patron saint. The physicians had St. Luke and the
soldiers St. George, but for the lawyers there was
no saintly head. Accordingly, he journeyed to
Rome and interviewed the Pope, who granted his
request, ordering that he should go round the
church of St. John de Lateran blindfolded, and
after he had said a certain number of specified
prayers, the saintly figure he should first lay his
hands upon should be the lawyers' patron. Evona
carried out his instructions to the letter, in the
presence of witnesses, and after some groping,
catching hold of what he thought was a saintly
image, he said, " This is our saint, this shall be our
patron." Then, tearing off the bandage, he found
to his horror that he had laid hold of the figure of
the devil under the feet of St. Michael. After
Evona's death, however, so good had been his
record, that he was himself canonised as the patron
saint of lawyers.

The generally accepted idea of a lawyer's progress is summed up in the three words, stuff,
silk and ermine, representing the barrister, the

King's Counsel and the Judge. An unkind critic, however, once declared that the three degrees of comparison in such progress were better described by getting on, getting honour, getting honest.

The spirit of antagonism that has always existed to a greater or less degree between the higher and the lower branches of the Law, the barristers and solicitors—due to the fact that one monopolises the higher posts while dependent for its existence on the lower—has been responsible for a fund of good stories. Once, in the hall of the Four Courts in Dublin, an attorney came up to a barrister (who hated attorneys) to beg a subscription towards the funeral expenses of a brother attorney who had died in distressed circumstances. The barrister at once tendered a pound note. " Oh, I only want a shilling from each contributor," said the attorney. " Oh, take it, my dear fellow," replied the barrister, " and while you are at it bury twenty of them."

This is somewhat akin to the story of the gentleman who had buried a relative, an attorney, and who complained to Foote, the actor, of the expense of a country funeral. " Do you bury attorneys here? " queried Foote. " We never do that in London." " Then how do you manage? " came the astonished question. "Why," said Foote, "when the patient dies we lay him in a room overnight, lock the door, open the sash, and in the morning he is gone." "But what becomes of him?" said the other. "Ah, that we cannot exactly tell," replied Foote, "seeing that we are not acquainted with supernatural causes. All that we know of the matter is, that there is a strong smell of brimstone in the room next morning."

But in this matter of members of the other professions poking fun at those following the Law, it happens more often than not that the lawyers score. "I say, doctor," said a lawyer one day, "why are you always running us lawyers down?" "Well, Brief," returned the doctor, "you can't say that your profession makes angels of men, can you?" "Why, no, doctor," came the prompt reply, "you certainly have the advantage of us there."

Where the educated man fails, however, it sometimes happens that the native wit of the street arab will succeed. "Please, sir," said a small boy to a leading member of the Bar who, in wig and gown, was crossing from the courts to his chambers—"please, sir, is this Chancery Lane?" "It is," replied the barrister. "Ah," said the youngster, "I knowed it was." "Then why did you ask?" queried the astonished barrister, receiving to his dismay the reply, " 'Cause I wanted to have counsel's opinion for nothing."

In connection with the relative precedence of the learned professions a good story is told of how the Law obtained the victory over Medicine. It happened that at one time a very lively dispute on this subject arose at Cambridge between the doctors of law and medicine, and ultimately the question was referred to the Chancellor of the University for settlement. " Does the thief or the hangman take precedence at executions? " was the first question asked by that official, and on receiving the reply, " The former, of course," he at once gave the decision, " Then let the doctors of law have precedence."

A fact not often realised is how much the Law owes to the wives of some of our greatest lawyers. For example, Lord Holt was said to have given his unwearied devotion to the Law owing to Lady Holt's nagging propensities. Judge Gilbert, who wrote so many excellent law books, shut himself up in his chambers in Serjeants' Inn for the same reason, and in several other cases of great lawyers their marked devotion to work has arisen from the same cause.

It has been said that only a fool goes to law, and though this statement is somewhat sweeping, yet

L—2

the vagaries of our laws are such that resort to
them is sometimes only justifiable as a last resource. There is more than a substratum of truth
in the dictum, that the requisites for successful
litigation are " a good case, a good attorney, a good
counsel, good witnesses, good jury, good judge
and good luck." One cannot but wonder what must
have been the opinion of our law held by the Turk
in a story told by Serjeant Ballantyne. The Turk,
an itinerant vendor of rhubarb, had been robbed
of all his earnings. The case was clear enough,
and the thief was ordered to be committed. The
Moslem was then told that he must appear to give
evidence at the next sessions, but he stoutly insisted that he could not, whereupon the magistrate
legally enough ordered him to find bail for his appearance. This again he was unable to do, and so
was committed to prison in default. In the meanwhile the prisoner had also applied for bail, which
was granted, and when the sessions at length came
on the Turk was produced from prison, but the
thief was missing.

On the other hand, there are some who go (or
are brought) to law with little hope of success, and
who find, to their astonishment, that they have
been successful. A certain man, who had a big
action brought against him, left the country as

soon as he had given his evidence, instructing his lawyer to cable him the result. To everyone's astonishment it was decided in his favour, whereupon his lawyer wired, " Justice has triumphed." Upon receiving this the defendant at once cabled back, " Lodge appeal at once."

II

IN THE OLDEN DAYS

It has been said that it is a very thin line that divides the saint from the sinner, and this appears to have been very true in times past as regards the Law, for more than one of our judges have in their youth been either breakers of the law or had some knowledge of the inside of a prison. Among others, Chief Justice Pemberton had in his younger days been an inhabitant of the Fleet Prison, while Chief Justice Popham was reputed to have been a highwayman, and certainly he acted with all the zeal of a convert, for it was a well-known fact that when highway cases came before him there was little chance of acquittal.

Nor did elevation to the highest judicial offices always bring with it a correspondingly high standard of conduct and morals. Among the articles of high misdemeanours presented against Sir William Scrooge, a Lord Chief Justice, we find the following: " That the Lord Chief Justice is very much addicted to cursing and swearing in his discourse, and to drink to excess, to the great disparagement of the dignity and gravity of his said place. He did, in his common discourse at dinner, and at a gentleman's house of quality, publicly and openly use many oaths and curses, and there drank to excess."

Avarice, also, appears to have been a quality not unknown among the judiciary. On the promotion of a barrister to serjeant-at-law, it was the custom for him to be presented to the Lord Chancellor by some other barrister, styled his " colt "; as he knelt down, the Chancellor attached to the top of his wig the little round patch that now does duty for the coif. The new serjeant then presented a gold ring to the Chancellor, another to his " colt," one to the Sovereign, and one each to the masters of the Common Pleas and the judges. At one ceremony, during the reign of Charles II, when seventeen serjeants were made, the Lord Chief Justice complained to the junior serjeant that rings given by him and the other sixteen serjeants weighed but eighteen shillings, whereas, according to precedent, those given to the Chief Justice and Chief Baron ought to have weighed twenty shillings apiece.

More than one judge has been well known for his weakness for a pretty face. A young girl, well endowed as regards looks, was arraigned at Leicester before a certain Chief Justice for stealing a pair of stockings. His Lordship, whose par-

tiality for pretty faces was fairly well known, calling the counsel aside, asked whether it was worth
while trying so paltry a case, and perhaps subject-
ing this young girl to the debasing influence of a
jail. In reply the barrister pointed out the duty
he owed to the prosecutors, who had instructed
him, and the necessity of making an example for
the protection of the town's chief industry. Upon
this his Lordship retorted that counsel " might
prosecute as much as he liked, but he would be
hanged if he would commit," and he was as good as
his word.

Barristers of those days were by no means the
quiet decorous persons that they are to-day, and
in spite of all the edicts of the Benchers, the fighting spirit would constantly assert itself. A striking
example of the lawlessness of those who lived by
the Law occurred in 1597, when John Davis, a
barrister, came into the Middle Temple Hall
during dinner with his hat on and a club in his
hand, attended by two others wearing swords.
Going up to the barristers' table, he hit another
barrister, Richard Martin, over the head many
times with such violence that the club was broken;
then, snatching one of his attendant's swords he
covered his exit from the Hall with it. For this
outrageous attack he was at once disbarred by

the Benchers, but was restored on petition four years later on his making public penance in the Hall and apologising to Martin. Martin later rose to be Recorder of London and an M.P., while Davis, despite his unfortunate early career, became Attorney-General for Ireland and Speaker of the Irish Parliament, and he had even been appointed Chief Justice of England, but died before he could take his seat.

Matters do not appear to have been any better across the Border, for, even at a much later date, it is related that at the circuit dinners at Stirling it was the custom for everyone to drink until they fell insensible under the table—the door being locked in order to prevent escape—and to avoid drinking to excess the only means to adopt was to sham drunk and roll under the table. Anyone doing so would there find a small pair of hands fumbling at his throat, and on enquiry what this meant a small voice would reply, " Please, sir, I'm the lad that loosens the neckcloths." It says much for the kindly forethought that provided a boy to " loose neckcloths " to prevent apoplexy.

As everyone knows, in these " good old days " the hanging judge was only too common, and so deficient in humanity were some of these gentlemen

that it is said of one of them that the only occasion
he was ever known to weep was when he went to
see "The Beggar's Opera," and found that Mac-
heath was granted a reprieve. Justice Buller, a
well-known hanging judge, was always said to hang
for sheep stealing, giving as a reason that he had
once had several sheep stolen from his own flock.
Another well-known judge, Justice Heath, who
apparently acted with more principle, used to hang
in all capital cases, declaring that he knew of no
adequate secondary punishment. "If you im-
prison at home," he said, "the criminal is soon
thrown upon you again hardened in crime. If you
transport, you corrupt infant societies and sow the
seeds of atrocious crimes over the habitable globe.
There is no regenerating of felons in this life, and
for their own sakes, as well as for the sake of
society, I think it is better to hang." Of another
judge, Sir Francis Page, it was stated that he
always felt it a luxury to condemn a prisoner, and
that on one occasion, when decrepit from old age,
he was asked by a friend in court as to the state
of his health; he replied with meaning, "Hanging
on, my dear sir, hanging on." In the same category also came Sir John Sylvester, Recorder of
London, well known for the violence of his temper
and his utter disregard of the rules of courtesy.

It was a favourite joke of this gentleman to call the prisoner's calendar his bill of fare.

Another excellent example of the rough language and rude mentality of the judges may be quoted from Justice Buller, who, when sitting in the Crown Court at Gloucester, once asked an obviously lying witness from what part of the county he came, and got the reply, " From Bitton, my Lord." " You do indeed seem to be of Bitton breed," replied his Lordship, " but I thought I had hanged the whole of that parish long ago." Another who earned notoriety in this respect was Lord Braxfield, a Scottish judge. To a prisoner who had very eloquently conducted his own defence, he said: " You're a verra clever chiel, man, but I'm thinking ye wad be nane the waur o' a hanging." On a second occasion, just as counsel for the prisoner was about to open his address, he muttered, loud enough to be heard by a considerable part of the court, " Ye may spare your pains, we're determined to hang the scoundrel at any rate."

In justification to some extent of these hanging judges it must be remembered that, living in our more peaceful times, we can hardly conceive the daring of the thief of a past generation. Once, while presiding at the Old Bailey at the trial of a thief, Sir John Sylvester happened to say in the accused's hearing that he had left his watch at home. The trial ended in an acquittal, and as soon as the prisoner was liberated he rushed off to the Recorder's house, and sent in word that he was a constable who had been sent from the Old Bailey for his Lordship's watch. It was accordingly handed over to him, whereupon he disappeared, never to be seen again. In view of the fact, however, that Sir John was a Jew, and a well-known hanging judge, there was perhaps some trace of humour in the theft.

When Lord Norbury was presiding in the Irish Criminal Courts, the Registrar complained that the witnesses were continually stealing the Testament upon which they were sworn. " Never mind," said his Lordship, " if the rascals read the book it will do them more good than the petty larceny will do them mischief. However, hang the book in chains, and that, perhaps, by reminding the fellows of the fate of their fathers and grand-fathers, may make them behave themselves."

As a result of this criminal daring, or perhaps as a cause of it, there existed a barbarous penal code, which, down to the commencement of the last century, prescribed the death penalty for nearly three hundred offences, embracing all degrees and varieties of guilt, and including such minor

offences as keeping company with gipsies, the picking of pockets to the value of twelve pence, shop-
lifting to the value of five shillings, robbery from
a dwelling-house to the value of forty shillings,
soldiers and marines wandering and begging without a pass from their commanding officer or magistrate, etc. These and many other trivial offences
were punished in the same way as the most cruel
and atrocious murder, and Mr. Townsend, the well-
known Bow Street runner, giving evidence before
a Parliamentary Committee in 1816, stated that he
had twice seen forty people hanged at one time.
The result of this severity was that juries, acting
on the principles of humanity, but in violation of
their oath, brought in the most ridiculous verdicts
in order to save prisoners from the hangman's
rope. Romilly, in his *Observations on the Criminal
Law*, published in 1810, quotes the case of a woman
who pleaded guilty to a charge of stealing two
guineas, two half-guineas and forty-four shillings
in money from a private dwelling-house. The jury,
in order to save her from the capital penalty, insisted that she had stolen only thirty-nine shillings.
In a second case a man stole goods from a shop
which the prosecution proved he had afterwards
sold for twenty-five shillings. The jury assessed
the value at four shillings and tenpence.

Nor was this barbaric code confined to adults, but it even dragged mere children within its scope. In 1748 Sir Matthew Hale ordered a boy of ten years to be hanged. Again in 1791 Joseph Wood and Thomas Underwood were condemned to death for stealing, neither being fourteen years of age, and the prosecutor only twelve. In passing sentence the judge declared that " it was necessary for the public safety and also as an example to other little boys to cut them off," and they were accordingly executed at Newgate on July 6th. A few weeks later another child of fifteen was brought to the gallows for stealing one shilling and sixpence, and as late as 1833 sentence of death was passed on a child of nine who had poked a stick through a patched-up pane of glass in a shop window, and thrusting his hand through the hole, had stolen fifteen pieces of paint worth two shillings. This the lawyers construed into housebreaking, the principal witness being another child of nine, who " told " because " he had not had his share of the paint." How great this scandal of child punishment had become is shown by a Government Return, which disclosed that in 1803 there were in Newgate as prisoners 391 children.

That the cruelty of our laws was not confined to criminal offences is even more clearly shown in the statistics of imprisonment for debt. In one year, viz. 1802, upwards of 200,000 writs were issued in England for the arrest of debtors for sums varying from fourpence upwards. Again, as late as 1792 a woman died in Devon jail after forty-five years' imprisonment for a debt of nineteen pounds, and, when a well-known philanthropic society, known as the Thatched House Society, set to work to release honest debtors by paying their debts, in twenty years they set free nearly thirteen thousand prisoners at an average cost of forty-five shillings per head.

The result of such a drastic code of punishment was that death became so common that it lost much of its terrors, and life to the criminal class became more or less a gamble. Death had lost majesty and even decency. This is well illustrated by the story of the Jew who had been condemned to be hanged and actually brought to the scaffold with a fellow-prisoner when a reprieve arrived. When he was told of this, it was naturally expected that he would leave the cart at once, but to everyone's astonishment he remained and saw his less fortunate companion hanged. When asked afterwards why he had not hurried away from what must have been to him a place of dread, he answered that he was " waiting to see if he could bargain with Mr. Ketch for the other gentleman's clothes!"

It is more than surprising on what slender pretexts some people will rush into law, but perhaps there has been no case to equal that mentioned by Dr. Nicholl, which, starting in the Archdeacons' Court at Totnes, went on appeal to three higher courts, the only question at issue being which of two persons had the right of hanging his hat on a particular peg. Apropos of lengthy litigation, it might be mentioned that the longest suit on record in England was one between the respective heirs of Viscount Lisle and Lord Berkeley respecting some property in Gloucestershire. Beginning towards the close of the reign of Edward IV, it lasted until the beginning of that of James I, when it was finally settled by agreement, after a litigation of not less than 120 years.

The conservatism which at one time characterised our legal system is perhaps nowhere so clearly shown as in the retention of "Ordeal by Battle" as part of the law of England until well on into the nineteenth century. The point arose out of the death of a village girl, Mary Ashford, whose body was found drowned one morning in a disused pit, bearing evident signs of ill-usage. Public opinion at once branded her companion at a dance the evening before, Abraham Thornton, as the murderer, and he was immediately arrested and tried at the Warwick Assizes in August 1817, but acquitted. As the Law then stood, a prisoner who had been acquitted might, in certain circumstances, be proceeded against by a process known as "appeal of murder," the appeal being lodged in cases of homicide by the heir-at-law. To this appeal a previous acquittal was no bar. Accordingly, Thornton was once more arrested and brought to London for trial, but in the meanwhile his counsel had been no less busy, and when asked to plead, the prisoner replied, to the astonishment of the court, reading from a slip of paper which his counsel handed to him, "Not guilty, and I am ready to defend the same with my body," at the same time throwing a large gauntlet on the floor of the court. Then followed long legal arguments, from which it appeared that the "appeal of murder" gave the appellee (or defendant) the option of challenging the appellant to single combat, the non-acceptance of the challenge rendering the suit void. Although this right had not been invoked since the reign of Charles I, it still remained good in law. The court thereupon decided that the appellant must either accept "battel" or the appellee must go free. On the same day that Thornton was discharged, the

Attorney-General gave notice in the House of Commons that he would shortly move to bring in a Bill to abolish this old procedure, and in the following year this promised Bill became law.

It is doubtful if anything would so amaze the old-time advocate, if he could be alive to-day, as the fees now drawn by well-known counsel. In the reign of Queen Elizabeth ten shillings was not thought too small a sum for an opinion given by Her Majesty's Solicitor-General. In fact, this was a usual fee, and gave rise to the common saying that " a barrister is like Balaam's ass, only speaking when he sees an angel." Among the records of the Corporation of Canterbury, it will be found that in A.D. 1500 they paid to three serjeants-at-law three shillings and fourpence each for safeguarding their civic interests, and about the same time paid the Recorder of London six shillings and eightpence, as a retaining fee. Moreover, in the sixteenth century it was, and had been for a long time, customary for clients to provide food and drink for their counsel, and this was regularly included in the bill of costs. Thus in the parish accounts of St. Margaret's, Westminster, there may still be seen the following entry: " Also paid to Roger Fylpott, learned in the law, for his counsel given, 3s. 8d. with 4d. for his dinner."

A perquisite of the law officers which existed till late in the eighteenth century was the free supply of Government stationery, not only to themselves, but also to any of their friends whom they chose to place on the free list. So great an evil did this become, that in 1733 Lord Chancellor King made a great effort to suppress the practice, with the result that he brought forth a gentle letter of expostulation from no less a person than the Archbishop of Dublin, who wrote as follows: " My Lord. Ever since I have had the honour of being acquainted with Lord Chancellors, I have lived in England and Ireland upon Chancery paper, pens and wax. I am not willing to lose an old advantageous custom. If your Lordship hath any to spare me by my servant, you will oblige your very humble servant, John Dublin."

Until comparatively recent years it was a regulation that Government officials, which, of course, included many minor legal posts, should not only conform to the established faith, but should take the sacrament within six months of entering upon office. A fairly well-known barrister, having obtained a small appointment as a local commissioner in bankruptcy, had forgotten all about this obligation, until one day, very near the end of the six months, it recurred to his mind as he was passing a church. Seeing several persons going in, he thought it would be a suitable opportunity to comply with the requirements of the office. Going in, he sat down in a pew and, without paying any attention to what was going on, busied himself with some papers that he took from his pocket. At the end of the service he went into the vestry and asked the clerk for a certificate. " A certificate of what, sir? " said the clerk. " Well," said the barrister, " I don't know much about it, but I have lately obtained an appointment, and I understand that it is necessary that I should get a certificate that I have attended what, I believe, is called the sacrament." " Sacrament," exclaimed the clerk, " why, Lord love you, sir, you've been churched."

The Bench and Bar of England, even in the days of silken ruffles, were well known for their sombre and sometimes sordid attire. In this respect perhaps the most prominent among a more or less dingy race was Lord Kenyon, of whom it was said that it was an open question among the members of the Bar whether his breeches were made of velvet or leather. It was further declared by the same authorities that the only handkerchief he possessed was one which he had found in the pocket of a second-hand coat he had bought. Running his Lordship close was Sir Charles Wetherall, whose clothes seemed to have been grabbed suddenly from some shop window in Monmouth Street without any consideration as to fit. He scorned suspenders, and only occasionally wore a waistcoat long enough to meet the other garment, which, for lack of the suspenders aforesaid, was wont to sink below the ordinary level. During the Bristol Riots he is rumoured to have made his escape from the fury of the mob in the disguise of a clean shirt and a pair of braces.

Apropos of clothes, an interesting survival of the days of old remains with us to-day in the shape of the black cap, used when the judge is about to pass sentence of death. This is a relic of the old coif cap, and formerly, when passing the death sentence, it was the custom of the judge to draw up the flat square dark cap that hung at the nape of his neck or the upper part of his shoulders. Having covered the whiteness of his coif, and partially concealed his forehead and brows with the sable cloth, he proceeded to utter the dread sentence.

III

THE HUMOUR OF THE BENCH

A JUDGE has very aptly been defined as a barrister who has been invited to sit on the Bench when he has had some considerable amount of standing at the Bar. According to another authority he is "the Essence of Infallibility . . . until the Appeal."

It is a peculiar circumstance that the one quality which is essential to success at the Bar, namely, that of self-confidence, is often for a time lost by the advocate when he is promoted to the Bench. It is a common saying that the fifteen years which a judge must serve to qualify for a pension may be roughly divided into three parts. During the first five the judge is always afraid that he is doing wrong; during the second he is always sure that he is doing right; and during the third he doesn't care twopence whether he is right or wrong, and then he is a good judge.

We have become of late years somewhat accustomed to the judge whose remarks are a more or less witty running commentary on the evidence, although perhaps preferable are those occasions when the judge scores off counsel, this being more of an equal battle. Of this the following is an excellent example. A barrister appeared before the Court of Appeal, over which the late Sir George Jessel, Master of the Rolls, presided. Counsel had prepared a most elaborate statement, and it was apparent that he had determined that it should be heard throughout. In vain the judge tried to put an end to him. Fresh point after fresh point was brought up, and the court had to listen. At length one was mentioned which Sir George pounced on at once, and said he would refuse to hear, as it ought to have been taken in the court below. "But, my Lord," complained the advocate, "I did take it in the court below, and the judge stopped me." At once Sir George was all attention, and leaning forward on his desk, he said earnestly to his tormentor, "Do you really mean to say, sir, that he stopped you?" "Yes, my Lord, he really stopped me." "Then," said Sir George, "you would much oblige me by telling me how he did it; the knowledge might be useful to me in the future."

A somewhat similar example occurred where a well-known counsel was arguing a long and dreary case of real property before Lord Ellenborough. Having not yet completed his case at the end of the day, he applied to know when it would be their

Lordships' pleasure to hear the remainder of his argument. "Mr. P.," said Lord Ellenborough in reply, "we are bound to hear you out, and I hope we shall do so on Friday, but, alas, pleasure has been long out of the question."

Another excellent illustration of a judge making a sly joke at the expense of counsel occurred in a case where an Irishman was on trial for murder, and so great was the feeling against him that his only hope lay in postponement of the trial. Accordingly, his counsel moved for an adjournment, and in support of it said, "With your Lordship's permission I will read the doctor's certificate." He then proceeded to read as follows: "I beg to certify that in my opinion if John Nolan is placed on trial to-day his life will be endangered." "Well," said the judge, "I do not wish to do anything to prejudice the defence, but judging by the depositions in the case, I should imagine the doctor's belief to be well founded."

Sometimes it happens that the judge is able to get in a crushing broadside on some advocate whose attitude to the court is not quite what it should be. When Sir Fletcher Norton, whose discourteous manners were proverbial, was pleading before Lord Mansfield on some question of manorial rights, to make clear his point he said, "My Lord, I can illustrate the point in an instance in my own person. I myself have two little manors. . . ." "We have all too good reason to know that, Sir Fletcher," interposed the Chancellor, thus wiping off a long score of discourtesies. In the same connection a good story is told of Lord Darling, who had asked a question of a leading counsel, notorious for his self-satisfaction. "God knows, I don't, my Lord," was the somewhat rude reply. "Is it really possible, Mr. Brief," quietly observed his Lordship, "that anything can be known at all that is not known to you?"

In the battle of wits that often takes place between the Bench and the Bar, however, victory does not always go to the former. Curran, the distinguished Irish barrister, was addressing the court at a county assizes, and it being a fine summer's afternoon, the windows of the building were open. At this moment a donkey in an adjoining field began to bray loudly, and the judge, interrupting Curran's speech, said, "Excuse me, Mr. Curran, one at a time, please." To this remark counsel simply bowed, and continued his speech. Later on, when the judge was summing up to the jury, the donkey came once more into action, upon which Curran rose and said, "I am sorry, my Lord, but there seems to be such an echo that I can scarcely

make out what your Lordship is saying." On
another occasion Curran having argued none too
respectfully before another Irish judge, the latter
at length turned on him and rapped out, " I am
afraid I cannot teach you manners, Mr. Curran."
" That is so, my Lord, that is so," came the
crushing reply.

An equally good story is told of that most sarcastic of judges, Mr. Justice Maule, who, when a
barrister, had to plead before Judge Taunton,
known for his brusqueness by the nickname of
" the Bear." " You are talking like a child, Mr.
Maule," said the irritable judge, " just like a
child." Putting his brief on the desk before him
and looking straight at the judge, Maule said with
the utmost gravity, " I don't resent being likened
to a child, for a child, if spared, becomes in process of time a man, but once a bear, my Lord,
always a brute."

It was the same judge, who, losing his temper,
unwisely barked out at a rising junior, " It's no
good your pursuing that line of argument, for what
you say goes in one ear and out the other." " Quite
so, my Lord," was the quiet reply, " what is there
to prevent it? "

Fortunately, however, the relationships are often
more happy, and the Bar is the recipient of a

humourous compliment from the Bench. Perhaps
of the many laughs that Lord Darling provoked in
his long career in the Law, none was so whole-
hearted as one that occurred in an action concerning the competence of an opera singer. In the
course of his evidence a witness said, " Well, I
won't say that the plaintiff could sing like the
Archangel Gabriel." "I have never heard the
Archangel Gabriel," remarked Mr. Duke, K.C.,
who was cross-examining. " Well, Mr. Duke,"
interposed his Lordship, " that is a pleasure still
in store for you."

It would seem, however, that in the days of old,
judges allowed themselves much greater latitude
than would be tolerated to-day. In a trial before
a well-known judge of the earlier Victorian era a
witness, Mr. Gunn by name, came into the box, and
owing to nervousness showed great hesitancy in
giving his evidence. " Come, come, Mr. Gunn,"
said the judge at length, " don't hang fire." Not
content with this, when the counsel had announced
that he had closed his cross-examination, the judge
dismissed the witness with the remark, " Mr. Gunn,
you can go off, you are discharged." Even more
rude was the remark of the judge in a case where
Erskine, acting as counsel for a lady rejoicing in
the unusual name of Tickle, thus commenced his

address to the court. "Tickle, my client, the defendant, my Lord." "Tickle her yourself," came the reply from the Bench, "you are as well able to do it as I am."

With every desire to be respectful to the court, it sometimes unfortunately happens that counsel will make some observation which had been better left unsaid. Here are two illustrations:

One Irishwoman was suing another for slander, and the plaintiff, when put in the box, was asked by her counsel to tell the court what the defendant said about her. "Oh, I cannot," she exclaimed in alarm. "But you must," counsel replied, "the whole case hangs on your testimony." "But it isn't fit for any decent person to hear," expostulated the plaintiff. "Well, in that case," answered counsel, "just step up to the judge and whisper it in his ear."

The learned judge had decided a point against a young barrister, and the youngster, somewhat nettled, imprudently said, "M'lud, I am amazed." His leader, fearing this might prejudice their case, hurriedly arose and interposed, "I must apologise, m'lud, for the hasty remark of my young friend. By the time he is as old as I am he will not be amazed at anything your Lordship does."

Next to the "scoring-off" of counsel come those

occasions when the judge rightly and severely deals with a witness who is not all that he might be. Though somewhat unusual, no doubt very successful in its result was the way in which an Irish judge once addressed a litigant who was obviously not confining himself to the truth. "Look here, sir, tell me no more unnecessary lies. Such lies as your attorney advises you are necessary for the presentation of your fraudulent case I will listen to, though I shall decide against you whatever you swear, but if you tell me another unnecessary lie I'll put you in the dock."

Almost equally obnoxious to the judge is the witness who puts on "side." Lord Morris, an Irish law lord, was trying a case where a veterinary surgeon was sued for damages for having poisoned a valuable horse. Among the witnesses was a dispensary doctor, whose testimony was to the effect that he had given 5 grains of the poison to a man without ill-effect and therefore 12 for a horse was not excessive. "But, doctor," said the judge, "wouldn't twelve kill the divil himself?" "I cannot say, my Lord," answered the doctor pompously, "I have never had the honour of prescribing for that patient." "Ah, no, doctor dear," replied his Lordship, "ye never had, more's the pity. The ould bhoy's still alive."

An equally good example occurred in a case where a well-known judge was trying a prisoner for stealing. Among the witnesses for the defence was a doctor, who said that in his opinion the accused was suffering from kleptomania, adding in a rather grandiloquent manner, " And, your Lordship, of course, knows what that is." " Yes," said the judge quietly, " it is what I am sent here to cure."

On the other hand, there is the rare occasion when the tables are turned, and the witness scores off the judge. A working bricklayer appearing before Lord Ellenborough, when Chief Justice, as a witness, came in his working clothes, and was soundly rated by the Lord Chief Justice for appearing in such attire. " I beg your Lordship's pardon," was his reply when the reprimand was finished, " but I'm every bit as properly dressed as you. You come here in your working clothes and I in mine."

One of the most pleasing characteristics of our judicial system, especially of later years, is the kindly attitude of the judges towards the juniors who are just embarking on their career. Perhaps in no other profession is this so markedly shown, and in this particular respect the junior barrister appearing before his Lordship for the first time

has much less need to tremble than the subaltern
in similar case coming before his general. Once,
when Mr. Justice Swift was presiding at the Old
Bailey, a woman witness continually addressed a
junior barrister as "my lord." At length the
counsel, looking at her sternly, protested, "Really,
my good woman, you must not call me 'm'lud.'"
"Ah," beamed the kindly judge, "you must not be
angry with the witness; let us hope it is only a
little intelligent anticipation."

In contrast to this comes an old-time story, told
by that well-known song writer and barrister, Mr.
F. E. Weatherley, of a judge in a certain trial who
consistently ignored plaintiff's counsel. At in-
tervals during the proceedings the unfortunate
barrister would arise and say, "But I represent
the plaintiff," to all of which the judge took no
notice beyond telling the speaker to sit down. At
length, stung to fury at this treatment, the counsel
jumped to his feet and shouted out, "But, my
Lord, *I* represent the plaintiff, and must do the
best I can for my client." "Quite so," replied the
judge calmly, "that's why I told you to sit down."

In another case a young barrister was making
his first appearance in court before the famous
Lord Ellenborough, and being suddenly afflicted
with an attack of stage fright, he commenced his

address to the court as follows: " The unfortunate
client for whom it is my privilege to appear, ahem
. . . the unfortunate client, my Lord, for whom I
appear, hem, hem . . . I say, my Lord, my unfortunate client." At this moment the Lord Chief
Justice leaned forward, and speaking in a bland
and cooing voice that was all the more derisive
because it was so gentle, said, " You may go on,
sir; so far the court is with you."

In the endeavour to impress upon a witness the
solemnity of the oath or the dignity of the court
the judge does not always manage to convey the
meaning he intended. Lord Eskgrove, a Scottish
judge, whose idiocies have become almost proverbial, once had before him in a trial for murder,
arising out of a duel, a lady distinguished for her
beauty. In administering the oath he addressed
her as follows: " Young woman, you will now consider yourself in the presence of Almighty God and
of this High Court. Therefore lift up your veil,
throw off all modesty, and look me in the face."

A somewhat similar story is told of Judge
Phillips, judge of the now defunct Insolvent Court,
who detected a witness kissing his thumb instead
of the Testament, it being a common idea among
a certain class that by so doing they were at
liberty to tell lies in the box without prejudicing

their chance in a future world. After administering a severe and thorough rebuke, the judge concluded with, " You may think to desave God, sir, but you won't desave me."

Sometimes, but very occasionally, it happens that the Bench will unconsciously give counsel a lead on which, if he is wise, he will not be slow to act. In his later years Mr. Justice Park had acquired a habit of thinking aloud, and during the trial of an old woman on a charge of stealing faggots, he unconsciously uttered the remark, " Why, one faggot is as like another faggot as one egg is like another egg." This observation was overheard by the defending counsel, who later, carefully and with emphasis, repeated it in his speech to the jury. " Stop," said Sir James, " stop. It is the intervention of Providence. That was the very thought that passed through my mind. Gentlemen (addressing the jury), you must acquit the prisoner."

Although we are perhaps inclined to look on judges as a race apart, yet we have to remember that they are but human, and sometimes very human at that. Sir George Jessel, Master of the Rolls, was a great equity lawyer, but he had one great fault in that he would drop his " h's." The stories of his difficulty with this letter were for years among the most treasured traditions of the

Chancery Bar. Perhaps the best relates to his dislike to Lord Chancellor Selborne, a very pious man, who had written a book of hymns. Seeing his bugbear approaching one day, Jessel turned to a friend who was with him and said, " 'Ere 'e comes, the oily 'umbug, 'umming 'is 'oly 'ymns. Oh, 'ow I 'ate 'im." It is related of the same judge that when he was told that a whale had been stranded in Oban, he said, " Impossible—a whale in 'Olborn! It must be a 'oax."

Another very human person was a certain Chancery judge, who was notorious for the brevity of his notes of evidence. The Court of Appeal had sent for his notes on a case which was to be heard before them, and, to their astonishment, they found that they consisted of a striking caricature of an oily-faced, evil-looking individual, bearing on top the words, " The Plaintiff," and underneath, " A blasted liar."

The best story, however, in connection with the humanity of our judges is one told by Serjeant Sullivan, the last of the King's Serjeants in Ireland, in his charming book *Recollections of an Irish K.C.* It relates to Sir Peter O'Brien, a Lord Chief Justice in the early nineties, who was always known as " Pether," even after he became a baron. In county Limerick there was at the time that Sir

" Pether " was on the Bench a lawyer who knew
the great man's weakness for beauty and liked to
play on it. In a hopeless case he put into the
witness-box as a last reserve a supremely pretty
girl. " Pether " beamed on her, but catching the
eye of a cynical bystander, his Lordship somewhat
quailed. " Mr. Kelly," he said to the subtle lawyer,
" this will not do. I don't mind admitting there
may have been occasions when testimony of this
kind might have affected me, but that is a long
time ago. Mr. Kelly, I'm now an extinct volcano."
This was disconcerting to the barrister, but he
noticed that " Pether " notwithstanding had commenced to ogle the girl, and the more she blushed
the more ardent he showed himself. " I dunno',
me Lord," said Kelly in a broad brogue, " but there
might be a few rumbles in the old crater yit."

Running this very close for pride of place is a
story told of Lord Chief Justice Coleridge, who
was well known for his grave and dignified speech.
Once he was sitting with a brother judge, when a
barrister handed to them a slip of paper containing
the name of the latest appointment to the Bench.
The promoted one was obnoxious to both judges,
and Coleridge's colleague criticised the new judge
in pretty strong language. The Lord Chief waited
until he had finished, and then turning to him with

L—4

a grave face, he said in his usual measured tones,
" I am not addicted to expressions of that kind
myself, but would you mind saying them again."
It was characteristic of Coleridge that he did his
swearing by proxy.

One cannot but think, too, that with a heavy
calendar to face some of our judges must at times
find the assize sermon tedious, especially when it
is long drawn out, as was the old-time custom.
On one occasion, when Lord Chief Baron Yelverton
was on circuit, an old college friend holding a
benefice in the town asked, and obtained, permission to preach this special sermon. It was the
month of March, the church was very cold, and the
discourse was tediously long. After the service
was over the parson, expecting congratulations,
approached the Baron and asked, " Well, my Lord,
how did you like the sermon? " only to receive the
reply, " Wonderfully, my dear friend, it passed all
human understanding, and I thought it would have
endured for ever."

No collection of stories dealing with humour on
the Bench would be complete that did not include
the classic one ascribed to Vice-Chancellor Malins.
At this period one of his colleagues on the Bench
was Vice-Chancellor Bacon, and a disappointed
litigant having expressed his displeasure by hurl-

ing an egg at the Vice-Chancellor's head, the latter quietly remarked, " That must have been intended for my brother Bacon in the next court."

Great as a judge may appear when on the Bench, however, in all the majesty of his scarlet and ermine, he often takes a different position when he doffs the judicial robes. Lord Brampton was once going into an assize court, carrying a brace of pheasants, and with his well-known terrier, Jack, at his heels, when he was noticed by a couple of workmen. " Gor' blimey, Jimmy, see 'im," said one of them to his pal, " the old bloke's been poaching again. See what he's got."

It was the practice of Lord Russell, after leaving the court, to drop into his club each evening for a game of whist. One night it happened that Fate dealt him a partner in the shape of a young guardsman, rejoicing in his new commission and a budding moustache, but who, as a whist player, was impossible. The game had not gone far before Russell was fuming, and finally he burst out with a torrent of angry expostulation. The guardsman waited till the outburst had ceased, and then in the coolest manner possible he leaned over the table and quietly said, " Look here, Russell, you mustn't talk like that to me, you're not in your wretched little police-court now."

In the same connection a very good story is told concerning Lord Alverstone, the Lord Chief Justice. He had been for years a member of Kensington Parish Church choir, and at the time that he was Attorney-General an American lady visited the church with the express purpose of seeing the distinguished lawyer. Drawing the verger aside, she asked him to point out the great man. " Well, ma'am," came the reply, " you see, there's me and the Vicar, but as for the choir, well, so long as they behave themselves we make no enquiries as to their antecedents."

Strange as it may seem, there are times when, even on the Bench, His Majesty's judges do not inspire the awe that we would expect. On one occasion when Sir Henry Hawkins, most sporting of all judges, was trying a case, the prisoner was observed to speak to the warder beside him in the dock. On this counsel for the Crown immediately asked that the warder should disclose what the prisoner had said. To this the warder demurred, but on receiving the judge's order to repeat the conversation, he announced that the prisoner had pointed to his Lordship and asked, " Who is that moth-eaten old heathen? I've often seen him hanging round the race-courses."

On the other hand, a hardened old criminal once

paid Mr. Justice Hawkins a very fine tribute. He
said if he were guilty there was no judge he feared
more, but if innocent, there was no one before
whom he would rather appear.

It is pleasant to note that the humour of the
Bench is not confined to the courts, but breaks out
also when its occupants have come down from their
high estate to mix with their fellow-men. Walking
one day through Regent Street, Mr. Justice
Mathew was accosted by one of the professors
of the bird trick, who, holding in his hand a painted
sparrow, began in the usual way. " Excuse me,
sir, but can you tell me what kind of bird this is?
I've just picked it up." Looking at the bird, and
then at the man, the judge replied, " Well, judging
by the company it keeps, I should say it was a
jail-bird."

On somewhat similar lines is the story told of
Lord Fitzgerald, a Lord of Appeal. He was approached once by a celebrated Jewish K.C., whose
complaint was that his undoubted claims to a
judgeship had been overlooked by the Lord Chancellor, Lord Herschell, who was himself also of the
Jewish persuasion. " But, my dear fellow," said
his Lordship in comforting the disconsolate one,
" what would you expect from a Jew but a pass-
over? "

Let us conclude with the story, which must, however, be given with all reserve, of the well-known judge who was walking home after a public dinner when an over-zealous policeman pulled him up and asked him his name. In his most dignified tones the judge in turn asked for the name of the policeman, and received the reply, " Paul." " Oh," said his Lordship, " I am indeed pleased to see you after so many years, but tell me now, did you ever get any answer to that charming letter that you wrote to the Ephesians? "

IV

THE HUMOUR OF THE BAR

NEXT to the perpetual conflict with the hostile witness the humour of the Bar usually arises from those cases where counsel, irritated by the Bench, forget for the moment the unwisdom of such a proceeding and hit back. It is doubtless a great consolation to the self-esteem of stuff or silk if they can pour in a crushing broadside on the irritable ermine, but, so long as human nature remains what it is it will scarcely tend to advance their client's cause. No more daring nor sweeping retort has perhaps ever been given in a court of law than that by Lord Russell, who, as a barrister, pleading before the Court of Appeal, when asked by a certain Law Lord for the authority for a proposition which he had brought forward, called out in his most rasping voice, "Usher, go into the library and bring me any elementary book on Common Law."

An almost equally telling story comes to us from the United States. "Mr. Jones, Mr. Jones," said the wearied President of the United States Supreme Court to a Western barrister who was laying down some very elementary propositions, " you must give the court the credit of knowing something." " That's all very well," replied the barrister, with real Western sang-froid; " but that's just the mistake I made in the court below."

For a direct reproof to a judge it is doubtful if any has ever equalled that given by the great Irish lawyer, Curran. Once when he was arguing in the Irish Court of Chancery before the Lord Chancellor, Lord Clare, he noticed that his Lordship, instead of listening to his argument, was fondling his dog. Seeing this, Curran at once stopped. " Go on, Mr. Curran, go on," said the judge. " A thousand pardons, my Lord," replied Curran, " I really took it for granted that your Lordship was engaged in consultation."

A somewhat similar rebuke was once given by Edwin James, a brilliant advocate, who later fell into disgrace and was disbarred. It happened that the presiding judge had interrupted James to ask several questions, with the result that the latter's cross-examination had been spoiled. When his Lordship had finished, James, instead of rising to continue, kept his seat, and the witness left the box. Then followed a long pause, terminated at length by the judge asking James if he had anything more to say. " Oh yes, my Lord, I have," came the cool reply, " but I am waiting for your Lordship to call your next witness."

Barristers, like concert singers, have, as a general rule, a great objection to any conversation being carried on while they are on their feet, and in this connection a good story is told of Campbell Foster, at one time a well-known barrister. Once, when he was addressing a jury, he was much annoyed by another barrister, Digby Seymour, who was at the same time carrying on a fairly audible conversation. At length, losing all patience, he turned round, and in a rich Irish brogue said, " Pray, Mr. Saymour, be quiet." " My name is not Saymour, it's Seymour," corrected Digby. " Then, sir," came the angry reply, " see more and say less."

A well-known modern lawyer who has made his contribution to humour under the same compulsion is the late Sir Edward Marshall-Hall. Pleading one day in court before a very deaf judge, he was much disturbed by a conversation going on behind him between Mr. Bowen-Rowlands and the leading counsel for the other side. Turning at last upon them, he said in a voice loud enough to be imprudent, " For heaven's sake stop talking; it's bad enough to have to deal with this deaf old man on the Bench." The roar of laughter which arose at this reprimand reached even the judge, who, holding up his hand for silence, and holding the other behind his ear said, " Hush, please, I must get that on my notes."

To one man in a thousand it is given to take liberties with the court, and to do this he must be a person of wonderful charm and personal magnetism. Such a man was Charley McKeand, at one time prominent on the Northern circuit. Remarkable alike for his readiness and resource, he was able to do the most startling and unusual things without incurring judicial rebuke. On one occasion he was given a dock brief for the defence of a woman indicted for larceny, and since he had come into court just as the case was opened, it was clear that he had not even time to read the depositions. A few words, however, from the junior who was devilling for him soon put him right, and he was quickly deep in an eloquent speech. At length, coming to the end of a really excellent piece of pleading, he exclaimed, " And what, gentlemen, did the poor woman say when the magistrate's clerk asked her for her defence? I will read you her very words, and I think you will agree with me that they bear the stamp of conscious innocence." In vain, by pulling at his leader's gown, did the junior try to stop this unwise act, but nothing could check the torrent of eloquence when once begun. " Let me read you her exact words. Ah, here we are. Oh, h'm." For a moment McKeand faltered when he saw them, but only for a moment. " Well, gentlemen," he continued, " this uneducated woman does not put it as you or I would put it, but I said I would read her very words and I will. What she says is, ' How the hell could I have taken the boots when he was wearing them ' and, gentlemen," continued Charlie in a concluding burst of eloquence, " I ask you, with every confidence, how the hell could she? "

Almost as great a liberty was taken by the late Tim Healy. He was opposed by Mr. Campbell, later Lord Chancellor of Ireland, who pleaded so pathetically in court for his client that he himself broke down and wept. Naturally, the Irish jury were much affected, as were the spectators in court, and moist handkerchiefs were to be seen on every side. With his opening sentence, however, Tim quickly obliterated the impression made by his opponent. " Gentlemen," he said, " the horrible details of the case have brought tears to the eyes of my learned friend. Really, gentlemen, we have not witnessed such a miracle since Moses struck the rock in the wilderness."

Sometimes it happens that the liberty is taken

with the judge himself. In this respect a good story is told of Mr. Justice Hawkins when, as a young barrister, he was once engaged in fighting a forlorn hope. In the middle of his address the judge interrupted him with the remark, " When you can prove that two blacks make a white, I'll listen to your argument." " I can do that, my Lord," answered Hawkins, " for I have known a black cock and a black hen to produce a white egg." An even better example perhaps comes to us from Ireland. Owing to accumulation of work one of the judges in the Four Courts decided to sit on Good Friday, notwithstanding the protests of the Bar. " Better the day better the deed," said the judge. " Well, my Lord," replied one of the complaining counsel, " you'll be the first judge who ever sat on Good Friday since Pontius Pilate."

Some strange defences have at various times been put forward by counsel, but the most eccentric of all perhaps was that put up to Lord Eldon, then Chief Justice, in a trial at Exeter Assizes. This was a case of riot arising out of a combination for a rise in wages among some tailors, and Mr. Jekyll, a prominent member of the circuit, was for the defence. The trend of counsel's cross-examination was apparently to elicit the number of persons present, and after this had been going on for some

time the judge reminded him that, as, according
to law, three persons constitute a riot, his examination was irrelevant. "Yes, my Lord," replied
Jekyll, "but these rioters being tailors there must
be nine times three, and if the prosecution cannot
make out that there were twenty-seven joining in
this breach of the peace my clients are entitled to
acquittal." The judge naturally overruled this
quaint idea, but it probably had some weight with
the jury, as they acquitted all the defendants.

Equally daring was Carter, a famous barrister
on the Western circuit. He was defending a man
at the assizes on a charge of obtaining money by
false pretences. "False pretences," he declaimed
with great scorn, "why, we all make them every
day. Barristers and solicitors and judges—the
whole lot of us. Talk of the purity of the judicial
ermine"—here he pointed derisively at the learned
judge—"why, it's only rabbit skin."

For the rapid smashing of an opponent's case,
however, the palm must go to Tim Healy.
This incident occurred in a case pertaining to
some timber, Tim being leading counsel for the
defence. In the course of the case a youthful
witness was put up as an expert on the plaintiff's
side. When the time came for the defending
counsel to cross-examine, Tim rose up and simply

asked two questions. To the first, "What age are you?" he received the answer, "Twenty-one," and to the second, "How long have you been in the timber trade?" "Two years." At once Tim resumed his seat with the withering remark to the judge, "A regular babe in the wood, my Lord."

Another remarkable example of the demolition of an opponent's case occurred in one where the Q.C. who was leading was called away directly after he had opened, and it devolved upon his junior, who had never had a brief before, to examine the plaintiff. Struck with fright the youngster stammered, stuttered, became hopelessly confused and quite unable to frame even one intelligent question. At this crisis the counsel on the other side rose quietly and said, "Let me put the question for you." The wretched youngster was too tongue-tied even to protest, and the whole examination in chief was conducted by his opponent, who then proceeded to cross-examine in the usual way, afterwards submitting that there was no case to go to the jury, to which the judge agreed. The performer of this remarkable feat was Mr. William (afterwards Mr. Justice) Grantham.

Extravagance of language is almost an unpardonable crime at the Bar, and it is doubtful if the story of one barrister noted for his flowery similes, and who later rose to the Bench, will ever die. When acting as counsel in an action for libel brought by a provision merchant against a local newspaper, he thus addressed the jury: " My client, gentlemen, is a cheesemonger, and the reputation of a cheesemonger in the City of London is like the bloom upon a peach, touch it and it's gone for ever."

Nor has the Bar failed to provide its quota of Irish bulls, of which perhaps the following is a unique specimen. "Gentlemen of the jury," said an Irish barrister, "it will be for you to say whether this defendant shall be allowed to come into court with unblushing footsteps, with the cloak of hypocrisy in his mouth, and draw three bullocks out of my client's pocket with impunity." "Gentlemen," said another barrister, "the whole subject is in the dark entirely till we come to the testimony of Mr. B. Then it is that the cloud of doubt begins to crack and the cat is let out of the bag." But the production of bulls is by no means confined to Ireland. Serjeant Vaughan, commenting on the evidence given by the opposing side, was guilty of the following delightful specimen: "And then we come to Brown. Ah, there the impudent and deceitful fellow stands, just like a crocodile, with tears in his eyes, and his hands in his breeches pockets."

in court was one given by a Miss Kennedy, Mother
Superior of a convent, from which a nun had been
expelled for certain breaches of the conventual
rules. In the course of his examination of this
lady, Sir John, afterwards Lord Coleridge, said,
" You say that amongst her offences was the eating
of a few grapes." " Yes," said the Mother Superior
quietly, " grapes were forbidden in a community
consisting of nuns who had taken the vow of
poverty." " But surely eating a few grapes is not
a crime? " persisted Coleridge. " That depends
upon the point of view," came the reply. " After
all, Sir John, we all know what happened because
a certain person ate an apple."

In the same connection a very good story is told
by Mr. Plowden, at one time the best known of all
London magistrates. Before his elevation to the
Bench, he was examining the wife of a notorious
burglar, and in the course of his examination he
said to the woman, " Knowing he was a burglar
how could you possibly marry him? " " Well, it
was like this," explained the witness. " Two chaps
wanted to marry me, and it wasn't easy to choose
between 'em, but in the end I married Bill here.
The other chap was a lawyer, same as you, sir."

There is also a very good story told concerning
that well-known critic and journalist, Sidney Dark

who had been called upon to give evidence in a case of theatrical copyright, the point at issue being how far one play was a mere copy of another. The opposing counsel, well known at the Bar for his somewhat brusque and rude methods, opened his cross-examination as follows: " You call yourself a journalist? " " I am a journalist," was the quiet reply. " Well," came the second query, " what sort of a journalist are you? " " I am afraid I do not know what you mean," answered the witness. At this the counsel, turning to the jury, sighed, with well-feigned sympathy regretted the lack of intelligence shown by the witness, and finally returning to the charge said, " I will put my question in another form, and then perhaps you will be able to understand. What would you say is your standing in your profession? " " I am afraid," replied Mr. Dark, " that I can only answer by comparison." " Answer any way you like, sir," thundered the counsel, " only answer." " Well," said the journalist, " I should say that my standing in my profession is a good deal higher than yours is in yours." At this reply a smile ran round the jury, which broadened into a grin as the judge quietly remarked, " You asked for it, Mr. Brief, and now you have got it."

A peculiar characteristic of members of the Bar

In view of the more or less peculiar circumstances in which the majority of the general public come into touch with the Bar, they are prone to look on them as beings outside the pale of ordinary humanity, failing to realise that they are very human and possess all the human failings. The common trait of impatience was shown at its best —or worst—by a certain well-known K.C. of the Midland circuit, Mr. Clarke. He was engaged in a case which the presiding judge thought a fit subject for compromise, and his Lordship accordingly made a suggestion to counsel on both sides to that effect. On one side there was no difficulty in accepting, but Clarke's client was obstinate in refusing, and held out for a long time, until at last Clarke, losing patience, exclaimed, " I'll tell you what it is, sir, you're a d——d old fool, and if you don't soon listen to reason you will compel me to use stronger language."

On another occasion at Warwick Mr. Clarke found himself opposed in a case by his son, also a barrister, and after the father had made some technical objections to certain matters on the other side, the son got up and said he would proceed to show the court how futile and utterly absurd were the arguments of the learned counsel on the other side. At this the indignation of Clarke père could not be restrained. Jumping up hastily, he exclaimed, " Sit down, sir, sit down; how dare you use such words to your poor old father." Forgetting for the moment, in his respect for his father, his duty to his client, young Clarke sat down until Lord Denman, the presiding judge, encouraged him to rise by telling him that his reverence for his father must not make him forget his duty as an advocate.

Of all the great wits that the Bar has produced none has equalled that prince of humourists, Curran. When going into court at Cork to prosecute a popular Cork citizen, Sir Henry Hayes, for abduction, an old lady said to him, " Good luck to you, I hope you'll win the day, Mr. Curran." " If I do," replied Curran without a moment's delay, " you'll lose the knight." As it happened, the result of the trial was that the knight disappeared from society for something like fourteen years. On another occasion a wealthy barrister remarked in his hearing that " No man should be admitted to the Bar who has not an independent landed property." " May I ask, sir," put in Curran, " how many acres make a wiseacre? "

It is recorded also how he had a dispute with a very tall and stout barrister, and, according to the custom of the time, challenged him to a duel.

Curran being of diminutive stature, the big man objected. " You are so small," he said, " that I might fire a dozen times without hitting you, but you can't miss me." " I don't want to take any advantage of you," replied the wit, " chalk my size upon your body and all hits outside the ring won't count."

It did happen, however, that Curran once got the worst of an encounter, and in that case his adversary was a well-known Irish priest. In the course of a conversation the barrister remarked, " I wish, Father O'Leary, that when I die you had the key of Heaven." " Why? " asked the priest. " Oh," replied Curran, " because then you would let me in." " It would be better for you," retorted O'Leary, " if I had the key of the other place, for then I could let you out."

Let me quote in conclusion one or two stories to illustrate the humour of the Bar when it is " off duty."

A barrister was once endeavouring to explain the success of another barrister when someone standing by asked, " Is ' X ' really such a great lawyer? " only to receive the reply, " Well, all that I can say about him is that his words always carry conviction—when he appears for the defence."

Another good story relates to Lord Chief Justice

Russell, who in his early days at the Bar was once asked by a brother barrister what was the extreme penalty for bigamy. " Two mothers-in-law," instantly replied Russell.

Of late years there has been a big onrush of students to the various Inns of Courts from our Eastern dominions, and in some cases they number nearly 50 per cent. of the students. In this connection there is a very good story told of a barrister going into the library of the Middle Temple and finding the place full of Indians. At last in one corner he espied a white man, and going up to him said in a grave voice, " Dr. Livingstone, I presume."

V

HUMOUR IN THE WITNESS-BOX

THE witness-box has ever been a fruitful subject for the legal cynic beginning with the one who defined witnesses as " persons on whom an advocate relies to prove his case—they lie, he relies." Perhaps, however, a nearer approach to the truth was obtained by a writer who stated that witnesses were of two kinds—professional and accidental— and then amplified this, in speaking of evidence generally, by saying that much truth was spoken that more might be concealed.

It is a strange fact that in no place are the distinguishing characteristics of sex so fully brought out as they are in the witness-box. There is an old and very true saying that in some respects the persons who make the best witnesses in a court of justice are women and children, the reason being that they do not stop to consider the effect that their answers may have on the case, but speak out just what is in their mind. Experience has shown, on the other hand, that they will tell falsehoods and stick to them in the most determined manner if they have made up their minds to do so. Another sex characteristic is that under cross-examination women invariably grow angry much sooner than men. The reason for this apparently is that the rules of evidence are particularly repressive of extraneous matter, and being checked in her flow of speech, a woman looks upon them as laws designed by man for the repression of her sex, and is accordingly hostile. She fails to understand why the opinion of her friend, Mrs. Smith, should not be a potent factor in the case.

A point which must never be forgotten, and one which applies equally to both sexes, is that for a time the witness holds the stage, and according to his interest in the case so does his pride rise or fall. From this circumstance it has been laid down by a well-known jurist that a plaintiff or defendant should be examined with more deference and ceremony than any other witness in the case. " They always feel," he writes, " that they are the chief actors, and are somewhat proud of having so behaved themselves as to have brought together a large number of people to listen to their mutual complaints and recriminations, and particularly of having afforded their counsel an opportunity of display. For all these reasons—in addition to their everyday ones—they are filled with a huge notion of their own extreme importance."

had been bound over at Ipswich, and called upon to find bail for good behaviour for six months. Then he would have turned to the incident in the double-bedded room at the Great White Horse at Ipswich, and bit by bit wrung from the wretched Pickwick the confession that he had been found in that room with a spinster lady. No, in the hands of a skilful cross-examiner, I am afraid that dear old Mr. Pickwick would have come out of the court with a very tarnished reputation, and one that would become ten times worse when the evening papers came out."

One of the most difficult questions that judges have to settle, perhaps, is the admissibility of children's evidence, the point being whether or not children understand the seriousness of the oath they take. A very good story in this connection is told by Mr. Montague Williams. A little fellow having been produced as witness, counsel for the prosecution suggested to the judge that it would be desirable to ask him a few questions, in order to ascertain if he understood the nature of an oath. His Lordship acquiesced, and addressed himself to the task of interrogating the lad. " Now, my little man," said he, " do you know what will become of you if you tell an untruth?" " Hell fire," said the boy without moving. " And what will become of you," continued his Lordship, "if you play truant and do not go to school?" "Hell fire," said the boy. "What if you don't like your brothers and sisters?" "Hell fire," again said the boy. In this way his Lordship ran through a long list of faults, many of them of a very slight description, but the penalty was always the same, "Hell fire." At the end of the examination counsel suggested that the little boy was hardly sufficiently intelligent or instructed for his evidence to be admissible. "Indeed," exclaimed the judge, "well now, I entirely differ from you. He seems a very good little boy, and if he grows up in his present belief, and thinks the direst punishment will be visited upon him for every fault he may commit, he will probably make a much better man than you or I." The boy was sworn.

A more up-to-date young person was the little girl who, according to Sir John Ross, late Lord Chancellor of Ireland, when asked if she knew what would happen to her if she swore what was untrue, replied, "Yes, my Lord, I would not be given any witnesses' expenses."

Unfortunate in the reply that he elicited was the judge who once asked a child in the box, "Do you know what an oath is?" and on receiving a reply in the affirmative, put the further question, "Well, what is it?" and to his astonishment, after some hesitation, got the answer, "You be damned." An Irish judge, also endeavouring to ascertain how far a child witness understood the nature of an oath, put the question, "If you don't tell the truth, where will you go when you die?" receiving from a child of ultra-Orange principles the crushing answer, "Where the Papists go."

Sometimes, also, in view of the mentality of the adult witness, it is necessary for the court to be assured that he or she understands the solemnity of an oath. "Do you know the nature of an oath, my good woman?" asked counsel of a lady who appeared in the box with an obvious black eye. "I did ought to, sir," was the reply, "which my 'usbind's a Covent Garden porter, sir."

A good story is told concerning two eminent Persians who were giving evidence in an English court with regard to a piece of machinery sold to an Eastern potentate. When the time came to swear them, it appeared that the only binding form of oath they acknowledged was to kiss the tail of a sacred cow. Then ensued a long legal argument as to whose duty it was to produce such an animal, but ultimately the matter was settled by swearing the witnesses on a reference library translation of the Koran.

Some people whom fate brings into the courts have very odd notions as regards the sanctity of an oath.   Mr. Montague Williams tells a story of one day attending a consultation in reference to a case that was to be tried on the following morning at the Central Criminal Court.   It happened that there were present two Hebrew gentlemen, who, for some reason or other, were exceedingly anxious that the prisoner should be acquitted.   During the progress of the consultation Williams had occasion to observe to the solicitor, " In order to establish this point we must swear to so and so," meaning it would be necessary to produce witnesses who could prove a certain set of facts.   Before the words were hardly out of his mouth, up jumped the two Jews —who could have had no personal knowledge of the circumstances referred to—and clapping their hats upon their heads, and raising their hands heavenwards, cried, " We swear."

A somewhat similar story is told regarding an Admiralty solicitor who was marshalling the evidence to be adduced, and worrying the witnesses in a vain effort to reconcile their conflicting statements. At last the captain of the vessel concerned in the case said, " It's no use to bother any more about it. Just you write down what me and the mate and the crew are to swear to and I'll see that it's done."

L—6

In the same category is the story of a dis
tinguished lawyer who was examining a Kerry
witness, of whose testimony he had grave doubts
Finally, he hurled at him the question, " Do you
know the nature of an oath, sir? " "I do, yer
honour," came the reply. " Are you not aware, sir,"
continued the barrister, " that you are commanded
in the Holy Book not to bear false witness against
your neighbour? " " I am, yer Honour," came the
indignant reply, " but sure, I'm not bearing false
witness agin him, I'm bearing false witness for him."

A legal cynic has said that " Many people kiss
the Book, thinking only of Ananias," and a famous
judge went nearly as far when he declared that
" Truth leaks out even in an affidavit." The point
has been well put by Mr. H. T. Waddy in the article
already mentioned, when he says that it is not easy
for even the most honest witness to be impartial.
" A person who is called upon to give evidence in
the witness-box almost unconsciously associates and
allies himself with the case of the party on whose
side he is called." An " independent witness "
(the proudest possession of the advocate) has been
known at the conclusion of the trial to say, " Well,
I'm glad we won our case." The allegiance may
be unconscious, yet it appears, and it is in conflict
with strict impartiality.

The great art of cross-examination is to know when to stop—that is, neither to ask too much nor too little—and it is in this respect that counsel only too often fail. The following story illustrates the danger of going too far. A policeman giving evidence was being strictly cross-examined by defending counsel. "What was the prisoner doing?" asked counsel. "He was having a very heated argument with a taxi-driver," replied the constable. "But that doesn't prove he was drunk," came the counter-challenge. "No," replied the policeman, "but there wasn't a taxi-driver there."

Another example of going too far occurred in a case where a witness had been called to testify to the supposedly high character of the prisoner. Having stated that he had known the prisoner all his life, that he was a man of blameless character and of great honesty, witness was asked by counsel as a culminating question whether the man in the dock was likely to be guilty of stealing money. "Well," replied the witness slowly and thoughtfully, "how much was it?"

An excellent example of a cross-examination not carried far enough occurred in a case where the only witness in support of a disputed will was a solicitor who had been struck off the rolls. Counsel in the case had full knowledge as regards the history of this witness, but being of a kindly nature he did not wish to emphasise the unfortunate witness's downfall. Accordingly, after the evidence in chief had been given, he got up and said, " I think, sir, you were at one time a solicitor? " " Yes," replied the witness. " And you are not a solicitor now? " " No," said the witness, and down sat the counsel, thinking that the jury would fully understand the circumstances and judge the evidence accordingly. What, however, they did in effect think was, " Here is a man who has retired with age and honour from his profession, and is probably now a J.P., so there can be no doubt about his testimony."

A good story of the same type is that of the old railway-crossing keeper who was giving his version of a night accident at his crossing. A gruelling examination only brought out the fact that he had waved his lantern frantically to stop the oncoming horse and cart, but all in vain. On the following day he was sent for by the superintendent of the line, who congratulated him on the way he had given his evidence, and commented on the fact that he had never wavered in his story. " No, sir," replied the old man, " but I was horribly afraid that the lawyer fellow was going to ask me whether my lantern was lit."

In another case the defence put up was that the accused, instead of being drunk, was in a state of considerable excitement, to which it was contended he was liable. In support of this an Irish doctor, a friend of the accused, went into the box. After putting one or two questions, the answers to which were satisfactory, the examining counsel asked, " Have you ever on other occasions seen the accused excited? " " Yes," replied the doctor eagerly, thinking he would clinch the matter for his friend, " frequently, even when sober."

It is very essential that questions should be put by counsel in the clearest possible manner, and not in such a way as to admit of an alternative answer. This is especially so in Irish cases, where the native ingenuity of the prejudiced witness will often enable him to foil counsel by an answer that, without being a lie, conveys a totally different meaning from the truth. In a county Louth election petition counsel was cross-examining a witness with regard to the distribution of free drinks to voters. " Did you give ' A ' a drink out of the motor-car? " asked the barrister. " I did not," came back the indignant reply. " Then did you give him a drink out of a tumbler? " counsel persisted. " I did, indeed," replied the witness in the coolest possible manner.

Another famous example of this occurred in a

will case, where the will was alleged to be a forgery concocted after the testator's death. O'Connell, the great Irish barrister, was retained in the case, and in his examination of one of the witnesses who had witnessed the will, the only answer he could get was that at the time the testator signed " The life was in him." " Was the testator alive at the time he signed the will? " he demanded. " The life was in him," came the reply. " Now," thundered O'Connell, " answer me at your peril. Was there not a live fly in the dead man's mouth when his hand was placed on the pen? " The witness collapsed, and immediately confessed to the trick.

One of the greatest trials to the examining barrister is the over-cautious witness. A man was on trial for shooting a number of pigeons, and the owner of the birds, a farmer, in giving evidence was so careful and so obviously nervous that defending counsel endeavoured to frighten him. " Now," he said in a fierce voice, " are you prepared to swear on your oath that this man, the prisoner, shot your pigeons? " " I didn't say he did shoot 'em," was the reply, " I said I suspected him o' doing it." " Ah, now we're coming to it," said the barrister triumphantly; " what made you suspect that man? " " Well," said the farmer carefully, " firstly, I caught him on my land wi' a gun. Secondly, I heerd a gun go off, an' saw some pigeons fall. Thirdly, I found four o' my pigeons in his pocket, and I don't think them birds flew there and shot themselves."

A carpenter, subpœna-ed as a witness of an assault, was asked by counsel what distance he was from the parties when he saw the accused strike the prosecutor. Pat came the answer, " Just ten feet five inches and a half." " Pray, tell me," said the counsel, " how it is possible that you can be so very exact as to the distance? " " Well, to tell you the truth," replied the carpenter, " I thought that perhaps some fool or other might ask me, so I measured it."

Almost equally careful was the witness in a story often told by Lord Brougham of an incident that occurred at York Assizes. In a case of assault and battery, where it was alleged that defendant had thrown a stone, the following evidence was dragged out of a canny Yorkshire witness. " Did you see the defendant throw the stone? " " I saw a stone, and I'se pretty sure the defendant throwed it." " Was it a large stone? " " I should say it was a largish stone." " What was its size? " " I should say a sizeable stone." " Can't you answer definitely how big it was? " " I should say it were a stone of some bigness." "Can't you give the jury some idea of the stone?" "Why, as near as I can recollect, it was something of a stone." "Can't you compare it to some other object?" "Why, if I were to compare it, so as to give some notion of the stone, I should say it were as large as a lump of chalk."

Many gems of humour, largely of the species of the Irish bull, are to be found amongst the evidence given in the lower courts. Here are a few examples:

Irish Constable: "After a fruitless search, your Worship, we found all the money with the exception of the silver teapot."

" I searched the prisoner," said a constable, "and found nothing on him; it was afterwards handed back to him."

" The prisoner said that were it not for soiling his hands he would kick me into the street."

" There were two of us alone at the time," said an Irish witness.

" The man was speechless drunk," said a witness at Highgate Police Court. "How do you know he was speechless?" asked the magistrate. "I could tell by his voice," answered the witness.

" The prisoner made no reply," said a police constable, "which I entered in my note-book."

"He fell on the road several times," said a witness. "He was so drunk that he couldn't keep his feet." "If he was so drunk," asked counsel, "how was he able to run after you?" "He followed after me between falling and rising."

"Were you in the vicinity of the accused when he committed the crime?" asked counsel. "No," replied the witness, "but I was standing next to him."

"He was sober enough to know he was drunk," was the conclusive evidence of another witness.

Even these bulls by witnesses fade into insignificance beside that of the Irish barrister who addressed the jury as follows: "There is no use in the learned counsel trying to throw dust in your eyes by dragging a red-herring across the trail"; or that of the barrister whose address ran as follows: "Gentlemen, the charges against my client are only mares' nests, which have been traced to their birth, and are found to have neither origin nor existence."

Bulls are not, however, confined to the Irish courts. Mr. James H. Campbell, K.C., in "The Times Book Club Case" asked a witness, "If the published book contained the unpublished part," a question which drew from Lord Darling the remark that " The learned counsel must remember that he was in England now."

Although cross-examination does not always seem to be material to the case, it is safe to assume that sooner or later its object will become apparent. Mr. Naylor, a well-known barrister, had been cross-examining an unhappy witness for twenty minutes on a subject which had no relevance whatever to the case. The witness was wearing a waistcoat of many colours, and counsel harried him with questions as to where he got it, what he gave for it, how long he had had it, and so forth, until the witness became bewildered and contradicted himself over and over again. Then Mr. Naylor appealed to the jury whether they could safely convict the prisoner on the evidence of a man who could not reasonably account for the possession of a waistcoat he was wearing in the witness-box, whereupon the jury found a verdict of " Not guilty."

In connection with this very common practice of attempting to discredit a witness a good story is told by Serjeant Ballantyne. He was acting for a Jewish solicitor, and it happened that one of the hostile witnesses also belonged to the Jewish race. Just as the serjeant was about to examine him the solicitor whispered in his ear, " Ask him as your first question if he isn't a Jew." " Why, but you're a Jew yourself," said Ballantyne in some surprise. "Never mind, never mind," said the solicitor with the utmost eagerness, "please do, just to prejudice the jury."

Not the least humourous situations occur when counsel leads the witness into a trap. The classic story in this connection is told of Daniel O'Connell, who was defending in a murder trial. The chief evidence for the prosecution was that of the bailiff of the murdered landlord. This witness produced a hat which he swore he saw fall from the head of the masked murderer as he ran away, and which he and several other witnesses identified as a hat belonging to the prisoner. O'Connell, with the hat in his hand, interrogated the witness. "You saw this hat fall from the prisoner's head?" "Yes." "And you immediately picked it up?" "Yes." "I suppose you examined it outside and in?" "Yes." "And I suppose you read on the lining" (here O'Connell, appearing to read from the hat, spelt out the prisoner's name). The witness, assuming he was reading, answered without reflecting, "Yes." "My Lord," said O'Connell, "I submit the case is ended. There is no name whatever in the hat."

A somewhat similar story is told of the late Lord Birkenhead in his early days at the Bar. He was acting for a tramway company, one of whose vehicles had run down a boy. According to the statement of counsel the boy's arm was hurt, and when he entered the witness-box his counsel made him show that it was so much injured that he could no longer lift it above his head. In due course " F. E." rose to cross-examine, which he did very quietly. " Now, my boy," he said, " your arm was hurt in the accident? " " Yes, sir," said the boy. " And you cannot lift your arm high now? " " No, sir." " Would you mind," said " F. E." very gently, " just showing the jury once more how high you can raise your arm since the accident? " The boy lifted it with an apparent effort just to the shoulder level. " And how high could you lift it before the accident? " asked " F. E." in the most innocent manner, and up went the arm straight over the boy's head.

It is a strange circumstance that lawyers' wills have always been notorious for giving rise to litigation, and that lawyers themselves only too often make bad witnesses. Mr. Montague Williams tells how on one occasion he had to appear on behalf of Mr. Justice Hawkins, who was prosecuting a man for threats, and, says Mr. Williams, " He who ought to have been a scientific witness was about the worst I ever had on my hands. Instead of giving simple answers to the questions, he did what counsel and judges always scold witnesses for doing—he made statements."

So long as human nature remains what it is, so long will attempts be made by witnesses to score off opposing counsel. There is an old, but none the less good, story of a duel between a K.C. and a doctor, in which the latter had to admit that sometimes doctors made mistakes, but he added to this confession, " So do lawyers." " But doctors' mistakes," said the K.C. in his most sarcastic manner, " are buried six feet under the ground." " Yes," replied the doctor quietly, " and lawyers' mistakes swing six feet in the air."

Equally good is the old story of the pipe-major of the Gordon Highlanders who was undergoing a bullying cross-examination, which culminated in his being asked if he had fought at Waterloo. " How cud I be fechtin," barked out the soldier, " when I was playing the pipes a' the time? It was mair wind nor wark wi' me, like a lawyer."

Sometimes the answer is of the purely impertinent variety, as in the case where Sir F. E. Lockwood was cross-examining a rustic. " What is the distance from one spot to another? " asked the great lawyer, and received the reply, " About ten miles." " Oh, you mean by the road; but how far is it as the crow flies?" "I dunnow," replied the rustic, "I never was a crow."

Now and again it happens that the witness, in his anxiety to triumph over counsel, only succeeds in turning the laugh against himself. "Where were you, and what were you doing?" asked counsel. "I was walking along the Eccles road at about four miles an hour." "What pace was the trap going?" "Very slow indeed, about three miles an hour." "Ha," cried counsel triumphantly, "but the trap overtook and passed you, you forget that." "I don't forget. It's you that forget. (This with indignant assurance.) The trap was trotting, I was walking."

Woe be to the witness who attempts to counter the searching questions of a skilful cross-examiner by a show of dignity or temper or both, for assuredly he will come to grief. In this respect Sir Edward Carson as an examiner perhaps stood supreme. "Do you drink?" he once said to a man whose manner was truculent, and whose nose suggested an obvious answer. "That's my business," snapped the witness. "Any other?" asked Sir Edward quietly.

Finally, there is the type of reply that throws an interesting side-light on how the other half of the world lives, or displays some little eccentricity that

convulses the whole court. " Do you mean to tell
the court that you came back to the works when
you might have been enjoying a holiday? " asked
counsel of a burly north-country witness. " Yes."
" Why did you do that? " " What else could I do?
I had nowhere to go. I'm teetotal now."

A lady defendant thus explained her action in
throwing soapsuds over another " lidy." " It was
like this, you see. She sez to me, ' You're no lady,'
and I smiles contempshus. Then she sez, ' You're
an outrageous female,' she sez, and I larfs scornful.
Then she sez, ' You're a woman,' she sez, and I lets
'er 'ave the soapsuds in her fice. 'Ow'd you like to
be called a woman, sir? "

The prosecutrix had a nasty wound in her head,
caused by a bucket thrown by the defendant.
" What have you to say? " asked the magistrate of
the accused. " How did it happen? " " Well, sir,"
replied the defendant, " she called me out of my
name, and I had a bucketful of water ready for her.
I intended her to have the water and not the bucket.
It slipped."

" What made you think accused was drunk? "
asked the magistrate of a police-constable, who was
giving evidence. " Well, your Worship," was the
reply, " she was in the middle of the road trying
to pick up the white line."

"He's the only one of my children who ever showed me any rale affection," said an Irishman who was swearing the peace against his three sons, "for he never struck me when I was down."

But for the brevity, which is, and always will be, the soul of wit, it is difficult to beat the following. Counsel: "Now, as a matter of fact, when expressing your opinion of the prosecutor you did use a little strong language?" Defendant: "Well, I don't know as I forgot anything." Or the policeman who gave evidence as follows: "I told the defendant she would be reported, to which she replied, 'Go ahead, my cheery little sunbeam.'"

VI

HUMOUR IN THE JURY-BOX

OUR essentially English custom of collecting a
number of persons of varied occupations, and for a
period making them supreme judges of vital facts,
is one that has met with a deal of criticism, but in
view of its long success it can well go on its way
undisturbed. Sir Archibald Smith, after he had been
five years on the Bench, said that day by day his
opinion of juries grew higher. "Sometimes," he
said, " I think that the verdict is wrong, and I feel
disappointed with it, but I think the case over, and
I find on reflection that the jury were quite right."
To quote a well-known legal writer, however, " The
system, like the British constitution, is a more or
less delicate piece of machinery, and there is one
thing that will throw it out of gear, and that is
bad management on the part of the person who has
to guide it. A judge ought not, of course, to be
a mere figure-head. He must have a mind of his
own, but then he ought to respect the mind of the
jury. . . . But where the judge deals fairly with
the jury, assisting but not controlling, influencing
but not dictating, putting the issue plainly before

them, and clothing what he has to say about the
law in plain language, the twelve good men will
very rarely make a mistake or cause the Court of
Appeal to be troubled." Indeed, there is perhaps
no British institution of which we can be so justi-
fiably proud as of our jury system, though few
would care to go so far as Sir Boyle Roche, when
he stated, in the Irish House of Commons, " With
trial by jury I have lived, and, thank God, with
trial by jury I shall die."

It is doubtful if the functions of the jury were
ever better defined than by the Irishman who, when
he was asked whether he was guilty or not guilty,
replied, " Ah, shure now, isn't it the jury that's put
there to find that out? "

Strange as it may seem, there still exists a certain type of person who fails to grasp the fact that
he is there, as a juryman, to give his verdict in
accordance with the evidence, but takes his place
in the box with his mind already made up, or with
a fixed intention to support one side or the other
" Have you no counsel? " asked a judge once in an
Irish court. " No, my Lord," replied the prisoner
" but I've several good friends among the jury.'
In another Irish court, no sooner had the jury
been empanelled than the prisoner excitedly
shouted to the judge, " Sir, I object to Mr. Clancy

serving on the jury." "Bedad, and for why, Michael?" came the answer from the jury-box, "I'm for yez."

It has been said that the jury's verdict is the expression of the judge's opinion, but this is not always the case, especially in Ireland. In this connection a very good story is told by Sir John Ross, the last Lord Chancellor of Ireland, in his book, *The Years of my Pilgrimage*. A judge, who was the terror of prisoners, came to the Assizes in a county where convictions were rare. A very clear case for the Crown was the first to be heard, and the judge delivered an overwhelming charge against the prisoner, in the course of which he remarked that it was the clearest case he had ever tried. Notwithstanding this the jury retired, and after an hour's deliberation returned to say that there was no possibility of coming to agreement. On hearing this the judge's comments were scathing, to say the least, to which the foreman replied that the majority of the jury were very sorry, but one of their number was holding out in opposition to the other eleven. Upon hearing this his Lordship wrathfully broke out with, "Then all I have to say is, that that juror is a disgrace to his county, and is shamefully violating the oath he has taken." At this a small bald-headed man among the jury sprang up and cried out excitedly, "I'm the man, and I'm the only wan houldin' out for your Lordship. The rest are all for acquittal."

In any case where the evidence is doubtful, to obtain unanimity among twelve persons must be exceedingly difficult, and one can sympathise with the foreman of an Irish jury who explained to the judge that there was no chance of agreement, seeing that he had eleven stubborn brutes to deal with.

Sometimes, although fortunately rarely, it has happened that unorthodox methods have been used to bring the jury into agreement. During the Bristol election of 1867 party feeling ran very high in the city, and some very serious rioting took place. At the subsequent trial Serjeant Ballantyne and Mr. Montague Williams were retained for the Conservative rioters, the principal prisoner being a solicitor named Watkins, who was very popular locally. The evening before the trial Serjeant Ballantyne was informed that a local butcher, a strong partisan of the other side, had declared that by hook or crook he would get on the jury, and that he "would have a leg off before he would acquit Watkins." Strange to say, the butcher did get on the list of jury for this trial, and Ballantyne at once challenged him, forgetting for a moment that he could only do this in a case of felony, and this was a misdemeanour. Foiled in this, he made an appeal to the butcher on the ground of his known statement, but Mr. Butcher refused to withdraw. The jury retired at 6 p.m. on the second day of the trial. About 10 p.m. they sent word to the judge that there was little likelihood of their coming to agreement. The Recorder, however, was determined that the State should not be put to the expense of a second trial, and informed them that it was his intention to keep them locked up for the night. About 1 a.m. they reported that they were still unable to come to agreement, and so they were sent back again. At 4 a.m. they said they had come to a decision, and the Recorder and counsel came back into court. When, in the usual course, the names of the jury were read over, only eleven answered, there being no reply from the butcher. Again his name was called, and this time there was a faint "Here." The Recorder wisely did not look in the direction of the jury-box; had he done so he would have seen the truculent butcher with his coat and waistcoat torn from his back, his shirt sleeves all tattered and torn, and his face covered with blood. The unanimous verdict was "Not guilty."

Few more agreeable methods of arriving at a unanimous verdict have been discovered than that employed in a case where one juryman wished to give a verdict for the defendant and eleven were for the plaintiff with substantial damages. After several hours of altercation, it was agreed to put four slips of paper into a hat marked respectively one farthing, fifty pounds, four hundred pounds, and one thousand pounds. The foreman then drew one, which proved to be that marked four hundred pounds, and the jury gave their verdict accordingly.

Nor have many people gone so far in their determination to stand out for a particular verdict as did one man in a special jury case arising out of an election, tried at Nottingham before Mr. Justice Littledale. After the jury had been called into the box and sworn, the leading counsel for the plaintiff rose and intimated to his Lordship that he wished a particular juryman to leave, as he (counsel) had been informed that not only had this particular person expressed his determination to find in only one way, but had also provisioned himself in readiness for a long sitting. On this the judge intimated to the offender that he had better retire, but as he failed to take any notice of the kindly hint, witnesses were called and sworn who deposed to hearing him say that he would find only one way, and that they had seen him put a soda-water bottle of brandy and water in his pocket, together with a large packet of sandwiches. This being found to be the case, the judge ordered the delinquent to quit the box, and further directed that his name should be struck out of the special jury list.

How far some members of the jury come into court with their minds already made up, without considering it necessary to listen to the evidence, is shown by an incident which occurred at York in a trial before Mr. Justice Gould. After the case had proceeded about two hours, the judge noticed that one of the jurymen was missing, and at once enquired the reason. " Please you, my Lord," answered one of the eleven, " he's gone away about some business, but he's left his verdict with me."

There is a good story told by Daniel O'Connell on this head. He was defending a man accused of murder, and so strong was the circumstantial evidence against the prisoner that it was clear the jury had determined upon a verdict of guilty. At the last moment, however, the man supposed to be murdered was brought into court, alive and unhurt, whereupon the jury were asked, as a matter of form, to return their verdict at once. To the astonishment of everyone, it was "Guilty." "What do you mean?" asked the astonished judge. "If the man has not been murdered, how can the prisoner be guilty?" "Plaze, your Honour," replied the foreman, "he's guilty. He stole my bay mare three years ago."

In civil cases, too, where the evidence is largely of a technical kind, and not easily understandable to the lay mind, the jury are apt to be more swayed by the personality or the eloquence of the counsel than by the merits of the case. In a trial at Merioneth, when the jury were asked for their verdict, the foreman answered, "My Lord, we do not know who is plaintiff or who is defendant, but we find for whoever is Mr. Jones's man." It turned out later that Mr. Jones was a well-known local barrister, who had been the successful candidate at a recent election, and that the jury had been working in his interest. In another case at Derby the verdict returned was as follows: "We knows nought about your plaintiffs or defendants, but we find for John Bogie," this, or rather John Balguy, being the name of a well-known sporting barrister engaged in the case.

Two other cases in the same county also gave rise to humourous verdicts. In the first, a case of petty larceny, the jury acquitted the accused, recommending his Lordship to tell him "Not to do it again." In the second, a man was accused of beating his wife about the head with a poker, so that she died. In the course of the evidence it was elicited that the deceased was of an aggravating temper, and was always nagging, and in these circumstances the verdict of the jury was, "Served her right." Neither of these, however, equals the famous verdict returned by an Irish jury which ran as follows, "We find the man who stole the mare not guilty."

It no doubt frequently happens, when a jury have acquitted a prisoner on the ground of the evidence being not sufficiently conclusive, and its members feel that they have won the accused man's lifelong gratitude, that they would be surprised to find that they have fallen very much in his estimation. An old criminal named Jackson was tried before Mr. Justice Hawkins on a charge of breaking into a country house at night and removing the family plate. He was found "Not guilty" by the jury. Some time later the judge, who had a remarkable memory for faces, recognised Jackson at the Bar Point-to-Point races, and entered into conversation with him. "You know, Jackson," he said at length, "that you were guilty of that burglary." "Of course I was," answered the "innocent" burglar, laughing; "your Lordship and me knew them jurymen to be a pack of blinkin' idiots."

One of the points which some counsel strive after most is to make the jury pleased with themselves, and from that to establish, as it were, a friendly relationship between themselves, their client and the occupants of the jury-box. Everyone will remember Serjeant Buzfuz's appeal to "A conscientious, high-minded, right feeling, etc., jury of his fellow-countrymen." Sometimes, however, carried away by his own eloquence, counsel does not quite convey the impression that he desires. "The principal fault of the prisoner," said one young counsel at the close of his speech for the defence, "has been his unfortunate characteristic of putting faith in thieves and scoundrels of the basest description. I have done. Gentlemen of the jury, the unhappy man in the dock places implicit faith in you." Equally unfortunate was the youngster, on his feet for the first time, who pleaded drunkenness as his client's defence, and began his speech with, "My Lord and gentlemen of the jury, you all know what it is to be drunk."

At one time it was the practice to lock up a jury without fire, light, food or drink until they arrived at a unanimous decision. On one occasion, when

Mr. Justice Maule, whose love of port was proverbial, was sitting, the bailiff brought word that one of the jurymen was ill and begged to be allowed a glass of water. " Let me see," said his Lordship, " water isn't fire, it isn't food, and it certainly is not drink. Yes, he may have it."

In connection with the right of challenging individual jurors there are many good stories told, of which, perhaps, the following is the best. In a case tried at Waterford the defendant exercised his usual right of challenge, with the result that among those asked to " stand aside " was a very decent, honourable man in the city—a citizen whose reputation for fair and square dealing stood very high. At the luncheon interval someone took the defendant aside and asked him why he had challenged Mr. ——. " Well, you see, it's like this," he said. " He's one of those men who would be influenced by the evidence." Actuated by a different motive, but even more wholesale in his methods, was an Irish colonel of Dragoons, who was defendant in a case during the old duelling days. Being told by his counsel that if there was any of the jury to whom he had personal objection he might legally challenge them, he replied, " Faith, so I will, and if they don't bring me off handsomely, I'll challenge every man of them."

Another prisoner went farther than this, for after listening to his counsel challenging the jury, he whispered to him in audible tones, "Challenge the old bloke on the Bench. He's tried me several times, and I know he's prejudiced."

The most common plea put forward to avoid jury service is that of deafness, but few have stated it so injudiciously as the juryman who, when he was asked by the judge, "Did you hear my charge to the jury, sir?" replied, "Yes, I heard your Honour's charge, but I couldn't make any sense out of it." He was excused.

In the Crown Court, on the oath being administered, a juryman addressed the clerk and said, "Speak up, please, I cannot hear what you say." "Stop," said the presiding judge, Baron Alderson, "are you deaf?" "Yes, my Lord, of one ear," replied the juror. "Then you had better leave the box," said his Lordship, "for it is necessary that jurymen should hear both sides."

VII

HUMOUR IN THE DOCK

THERE are few words in the English language that carry with them the sorrow and the pathos of that simple one " dock." It is above all a place of extremes, at one moment the centre of a ripple of laughter, at another a place of tragedy too deep even for utterance. At one time it will hold one to whom the world has given little, at another someone to whom Fate has been more than generous in her gifts. " But what are the people like who commit crimes? " asks Mr. Cairns, the Metropolitan magistrate, in his delightful book, *The Loom of the Law*. " They seem to be just ordinary folk—just like you and me. Every class and order, every trade and profession, every age and temperament make their contribution to the children of sorrow. Saints and sinners, preachers and pawnbrokers, tradesmen and bookies, ladies of much leisure and ladies of little virtue . . . and little children. Prosperity and poverty, culture and coarseness, Literature and Art and Science, Army and Navy and Law, Church and State—all have a place in the dock. It is the most democratic institution in the world. The vista of the dock is the final vision of our common frailty. On the same rail there rests the hands of our complex and bewildered humanity, some gloved in kid and some in grime and blood."

In every court of justice the dock occupies the most important if not the most honourable position, for it is the point on which all eyes are turned. Its occupants are ever changing, and the sad and continuous pilgrimage from the cell to the dock provides a kaleidoscope of human emotions which few can witness unmoved. In the figures that enter there, stay for a time, and then disappear, we see an exhibition of the follies, the frailties and the passions of human nature that cannot be equalled elsewhere. It is the way of grief and pain, and the travellers on that road are only too numerous.

The ability of the prisoner to give evidence on his own behalf has transferred a great deal of humour from the dock to the witness-box, but even now at times it flashes forth to convulse the court. Perhaps the most fruitful source is the prisoner who unwittingly gives away his own case. A prisoner was charged in a Scottish court with pocket picking. To all of the prosecution he listened with the greatest indifference, but when his counsel rose to address the jury he became very interested. In the course of his address counsel endeavoured to discredit the evidence for the prosecution, and warming to his subject exclaimed, " If this young man had taken the money, where, I ask, could he have placed it? Not in his pockets, for they would, of course, be examined at once. Not in his shoes, for they also would be inspected. Where, then, gentlemen of the jury, could this lad have stored the money? Where was there a place he could have found to store it away? " At this point the counsel made a long and dramatic pause, and the prisoner, thinking he wanted assistance, exclaimed, pointing to an inside pocket, " I put it in here, sir."

Another story concerns a prisoner who was on his trial at the Quarter Sessions for the crime of stealing ducks. His counsel addressed the jury at great length, pointing out firstly, that it had not been conclusively proved that the prosecutor had lost any ducks; secondly, that the ducks found in the prisoner's cottage were not those of the prosecutor; and thirdly, that the prisoner had established an absolute alibi. Just as the chairman began to sum up the prisoner interposed and asked if he might say something, and, as an indulgence, this was permitted. " All I want to say, gentlemen," he remarked, " is that I wish I'd never seen the d——d ducks."

An excellent example of a prisoner giving away his own case occurred in a trial before Baron Parke at Leicester Assizes. The accused was charged with cutting and wounding with intent, and addressing the judge and jury on his own behalf, he endeavoured to point out that he was by nature a peaceable man. " Now, my Lord," he expostulated, " I've been called a quarrelsome man, but that's a downright falsity, for look here, how can I be a quarrelsome man when I've been bound over twenty-three times to keep the peace? "

The idea of some prisoners that they can conduct their defence better than counsel sometimes leads to humourous situations, but few have gone as far in their egoism as the old criminal who, having asked for legal assistance, was told by the judge to " Look at those gentlemen of the Bar and choose the one whom you prefer." The prisoner scanned the faces of the counsel intently for a few moments, and then turning back to the judge said forlornly, " I think I'd better defend myself, my Lord." For tactlessness also it would be difficult to beat the case of the man who, when asked if he wished to be defended by counsel, replied, " No, my Lord, I'm going to throw myself upon the ignorance of the court."

The classic example of a prisoner giving away

his own case, through his desire to supplement the efforts of his counsel, occurred in a trial before Lord Russell of Killowen when Lord Chief Justice. The prisoner was indicted for a very serious crime, and the evidence against him was so overwhelming that his case was hopeless, but he insisted on supplementing the speech of his somewhat inexperienced counsel by delivering one on his own account. At first he was fairly understandable in his endeavour to assure the court that this was the first time he had ever been in the hands of the police, but soon the novelty of his position overcame him, and words failed him, until at length he became absolutely incoherent. With admirable patience the Lord Chief Justice listened to him until the words became a mere jumble, when, leaning forward he said, " What was your last sentence? " and to the astonishment of the whole court the prisoner, who had entirely misunderstood the meaning of the question, replied, " Seven years, my Lord."

There is a type of cheerful impertinence heard in the dock which does much to relieve the tedium of the courts. Here are a few examples.

" What brings you here again? " asked a magistrate of an old offender, only to receive the reply, " Force of 'abit."

L—8

An Irishman was charged with bigamously marrying no fewer than five women, and when the magistrate asked him how he could be so hardened a villain, he replied, " Please, your Worship, I was trying to get a good one."

The prisoner was an old offender, not unknown to the judge who was trying him. " It is time you were checked in your career of crime," said his Lordship. " How many times have you been convicted of this offence before? " " Five, my Lord," was the quiet reply. " Five," said his Lordship, " then this time I shall give you the maximum sentence laid down by the law." " Maximum," echoed the prisoner, " don't regular customers get a bit of discount? "

For real native humour there is nothing to beat the story of the woman who was prosecuted before a Dublin magistrate for disorderly conduct and resisting arrest. Being asked by the magistrate if she had anything to say in her defence, she replied, with an arch look at the good-looking young constable who had arrested her, " I lave it to yourself, yer Honour, if anyone could resist that young man."

Although obviously intended to be impertinent, the defence of the prisoner who pleaded guilty to making counterfeit money might be excused on

account of its humour. " The fact is, your Lordship," he pleaded in extenuation, "the supply
of the genuine article is so limited, and
things is generally so tight, a poor fellow must
do something these times to turn an honest
penny."

Perhaps the greatest terror to the court is " the
habitual," who, with little hope of a light sentence,
and realising that for a few moments he (or she)
holds the stage, is determined to make the most of
it. Such a person was Mrs. Mary Matthews, who
some twenty years ago signalised her fifty-second
appearance by considerably enlivening the
Clerkenwell Sessions Court. Knowing by experience the dullness of the court procedure, she opened
the proceedings by singing, " Mary was young and
fair and Mary had golden hair," at the same time
shaking her copper-coloured tresses. The row of
counsel then catching her eye, she executed a little
dance, warbling, " Jig-a-jig, jig, jig-a-jig, jig, a nice
little man in a nice little wig." Her invitation to
what she called the " Wiggies " (the barristers) to
come and have a quiet musical meeting met with
no response, and the attempt of the presiding
magistrate to quieten her only brought forth the
song, " You can't keep me quiet, if you try there'll
be a riot," followed after a second attempt by, " Oh,

dear, oh, dear, do let me be, for I'm certain we shall never agree." In the end Mrs. Matthews had to be led below.

A similar story is told by Mr. Cairns, concerning an old Irishman who made his third appearance for drunkenness within a week. He went into the dock, but to the question of " Guilty or not guilty " he paid no attention, his mind seeming to be engaged in some matter much more important than the charge. Once more the jailer put the question, and with a wave of his hand, as though brushing aside some triviality, the Irishman said, " Of course I'm guilty," and proceeded to address the magistrate on a much more important topic in a brogue that was certainly bred in the neighbourhood of Blarney. " Do you know, sorr, it's six and thirty years since I came to this country, and plaze God this time next year I'll be back in county Cork. I think, sorr, the Treaty will be ratified sure enough, and it will be a great day for everyone concerned when . . ." Here the magistrate intervened, and reminded him of the little matter that was charged against him. " He looked," said Mr. Cairns, " grieved and surprised that I had failed to appreciate matters of real importance, and it was clear I had fallen in his esteem." He replied, " Och, sure, that's only a trifle. What do ye say to five shillings? " I reminded him that it was his third appearance. "Och, shure, the whole thing's not worth talking about. I'll lave the five shillings with the jailer." And he did.

In an attempt to assist the prisoner in his defence, the judge or magistrate will sometimes elicit real gems of humour. "Your case would have been stronger," said the magistrate to a man summoned for assault, "if you had acted on the defensive, but according to the evidence you struck first. If you had let him strike first you would have had the law on your side." "Yes," said the defendant sadly, "I should have had the law on my side, but I should have had Ryan on my stomach." In a second case, tried before the Recorder of Dublin, a man was charged with stealing the contents of the till of a small sweet shop, which contents only amounted to sevenpence halfpenny. "It's a sad thing," said the Recorder, "to see a young man of your age losing character and prospects for sevenpence halfpenny." "Shure now, my Lord, that's not my fault at all," said the prisoner. "It wasn't your fault," said the Recorder, hoping to hear something that would justify him in passing a light sentence. "No, me Lordship. How was I to consave that there'd be only a dhirty seven-

pence halfpenny in the d——d till? Didn't I clane
out every blessed farthing I could find?"

In this connection perhaps the best story is one
told by the great humourist, Pett Ridge, in his
book, *I Like to Remember*. A magistrate wishing
to show leniency determined to bind a prisoner
over, and asked him if he had any friends who
would act as sureties. "The Almighty is my
friend," shouted the defendant. "Yes, yes," replied
the magistrate, "but the point is, can you give us
the name of a friend living near?" "The Almighty
is everywhere," answered the man. "I know,"
said the magistrate patiently, "but I am afraid
we shall have to think of someone of more settled
habits."

Strange and wonderful have been the defences
that have from time to time been put forward from
the dock, and one of the most successful comes to
us from America. Defendant, a tough-looking
fellow, was charged with driving at an excessive
speed. "The evidence shows that you were going
at sixty miles an hour," said the judge. "What's
your explanation for going at such a whiz?"
"Waal, ye see, judge," replied the accused, "I just
had to skip along lively 'cause I'd pinched the
car." "Sure," said the judge, "that's reasonable.
Case dismissed."

There are many good stories concerning the dissatisfaction of prisoners with their counsel, but few where they express their approbation of his efforts. On one occasion, however, a prisoner, having pleaded guilty, his counsel addressed the court with such skill that the prisoner interposed and asked to be allowed to withdraw his plea, as having heard his counsel's speech he was now persuaded of his own innocence.

Somewhat embarrassing was the gratitude of an old pickpocket whose acquittal had been secured by the advocacy of Montague Williams. Waylaying the distinguished counsel outside the Old Bailey, the old rascal said, " Gawd bless yer, guv'nor. I ain't paid you half enough for what you've done for me, but if you'll come along to Piccadilly and choose a little bit of jewellery, watch and chain or ring, I'll get it for you without any difficulty."

Out of the same feeling of gratitude, O'Connell, the great Irish lawyer, was given a piece of illicit but useful knowledge, but whether or not he made use of it history does not record. He had defended a man accused of cattle stealing, and owing to a flaw in the indictment had obtained an acquittal. In the course of the evidence it came out that the animal in question was the fattest of all the cows in the field, and that the night on which it was stolen was as dark as pitch. The same evening the grateful cattle stealer came round to O'Connell's lodging to thank him for having saved his life—for in those days cattle stealing was a capital offence. "But how in the world," asked O'Connell, "did you contrive to pick out the fattest cow when the night was quite dark?" "Well, your honour," replied the guiltless one, "you saved my life, so I'll put you up to the dodge. When you go to steal a cow always take the best, for if you're in for a penny you may as well be in for a pound. To do this always take her that's on the inside; the wakest creatures always make for the ditch for shelter, but the fat bastes are always to be found in the centre of the field."

For callous comment on the efforts of his counsel there has been perhaps none to equal that of a certain illiterate prisoner who was being tried for murder. The Crown provided him with a young counsel who made a most touching appeal on behalf of his poor helpless client. The young barrister's speech to the jury was so pathetic that when he sat down the jury were shedding tears, the judge had his handkerchief out, and ladies were weeping all over the court. When counsel resumed his seat, the prisoner turned to the warder with the query, "Who's that bloke that has been talking?" "That's your counsel," said the warder, "he has been pleading for your life." "Ain't he a dismal bounder?" was the reply.

eyebrows and remarking, " Well, gentlemen." This was almost equalled by Baron Bramwell on an occasion where the defendant's counsel closed his case without calling a witness whose evidence would have been very material to the issue, and whose coming had been eagerly awaited. " Aren't you calling Jones, Mr. Bigwig? " asked his Lordship significantly. " I am not, my Lord," replied the advocate. " Whew," whistled the Baron. " Gentlemen, consider your verdict." Mr. Justice Hawkins summing up in a larceny case, although somewhat longer, would be difficult to beat for terseness and sarcasm, " Gentlemen of the jury," he said, " the prisoner said he didn't steal the candlesticks, and six witnesses said he did. It is for you to decide who are the liars."

Of all His or Her Majesty's judges who have contributed to the humour of the summing-up, undoubtedly Mr. Justice Maule takes first place. His humour, although sometimes slightly coarse, was always genuine and amusing, and of sarcasm he was a past master. The following is an excellent example occurring in a case in which there had been some hard swearing on both sides. " Gentlemen of the jury," he said, " if you believe the witnesses for the plaintiff you will find for the plaintiff. If you believe the witnesses for the defendant, you will find for the defendant. If, like myself, you don't believe any of them, Heaven knows which way you will find. Consider your verdict."

Another example of his quiet sarcasm occurred in a libel case in which the defending barrister finished a flamboyant and grandiloquent speech with the statement, " This, gentlemen, is a shameful, an infamous, nay, I may say a diabolical prosecution." " Gentlemen of the jury," said Maule at the end of his summing-up, " you are told that this is a diabolical prosecution, but, gentlemen, you must give the devil his due and find the defendant guilty," which they did.

Perhaps his best effort, however, was directed against the existing divorce law which at that time made divorce a luxury for the rich only. A prisoner having been found guilty of bigamy, the following conversation took place.

Clerk of Assize: " What have you to say that judgment should not be passed upon you according to law? "

Prisoner: " Well, my Lord, my wife took up with a hawker and ran away five years ago; and I have never seen her since, so I married this other woman last winter."

Justice Maule: " Prisoner at the Bar, I will tell you what you ought to have done, and if you say you did not know, I must tell you that the Law conclusively presumes that you did. You ought to have instructed your attorney to bring an action against the hawker for criminal conversation with your wife. That would have cost you about £100. When you had recovered substantial damages against the hawker, you would have instructed your proctor to sue in the ecclesiastical courts for a divorce *a mensa atque thoro*. That would have cost you £200 or £300 more. When you had obtained a divorce *a mensa atque thoro*, you would have had to appear by counsel before the House of Lords for a divorce *a vinculo matrimonii*. The Bill might have been opposed in all its stages in both Houses of Parliament, and altogether you would have had to spend about £1,000 or £1,200. You will probably tell me that you never had 1,000 farthings of your own in the world, but, prisoner, that makes no difference. Sitting here as a British judge, it is my duty to tell you that this is not a country in which there is one law for the rich and another for the poor."

Worthy of a high place among brief and witty summings-up is one made by Baron Alderson in an obvious case of guilt, where the employment of counsel for the defence would have been a sheer waste of time and money. Addressing the prisoner, who was charged with the theft of a pair of shoes, he said in a kindly tone, " Tell the jury all about it." " Well, my Lord, it was like this," said the man. " I was walking past the shop when I saw the shoes, and it occurred to me that I might have a bit of fun with the shopkeeper, so I waited until his back was turned and I just took them." " Is that your defence? " asked Alderson. " Yes, my Lord, I took the shoes as a practical joke." " And how far did you carry them? " said his Lordship benignly. " A matter of two miles, my Lord," was the reply. The judge turned to the jury, " I think that is carrying the joke too far. What do you say, gentlemen? " Even more damning was the summing-up of an Irish judge who, in a trial for murder, is reported to have briefly closed the trial with the following words, " Well, gentlemen, after this evidence we must drop the subject."

Sometimes it happens that, almost of necessity, the judge in his summing-up is forced through the extravagant defence of counsel to resort to irony or sarcasm. In this connection a good story is told by Mr. Plowden. He had been retained to defend a man on a charge of horse stealing, and during his temporary absence from the court, the man pleaded guilty. Learning what had happened on his return, Plowden saw the judge, and asked him privately to allow the plea to be withdrawn, and after some demur this was allowed. At the conclusion of the case Mr. Plowden made a most impassioned address to the jury, and then the judge summed up. " Gentlemen of the jury," he said, " the prisoner at the Bar is indicted for stealing a horse. To this charge he has pleaded guilty, but his learned counsel is convinced that this was a mistake. The question is one, therefore, for you gentlemen which you will believe. If you should have any doubt, pray bear this in mind, that the prisoner was there, and the learned counsel wasn't."

Less successful in his use of sarcasm, however, was the late Lord Bowen. He was once, says Mr. Bowen Rowlands in *In Court and out of Court,* presiding over an Assize Court, and the case was one of a man charged with burglary. It was proved in evidence that the burglar had broken into the house, and was discovered on the roof with his boots hanging round his neck and the valuables in a sack in his possession. The defence was that he had seen the door open, entered the house and gone on to the roof with no felonious purpose. Bowen, in his most sarcastic vein, informed the jury that if they considered that the man's presence on the roof was due to a love of fresh air, that he had removed his boots in order not to disturb the rest of the members of the household, and that the presence of the valuables in a sack was explainable by the fact that he wished to remove them to a place of safety and would bring them back later, then they would acquit the prisoner. Taking the judge at his word, the jury accordingly acquitted him.

Sometimes in the olden days, it happened that the judge was not above allowing his own personal feelings to come to the front in his summing-up. " I remember well," says Charles Phillips in *Curran and his Contemporaries,* " at the Sligo Summer Assizes for 1812, being of counsel in the case of the King *v.* Fenton for the murder of Major Hillas in a duel, when Judge Fletcher thus capped his summing-up to the jury. ' Gentlemen, it's my business to lay down the Law to you, and I will. The Law says the killing of a man in a duel is murder, therefore, in the discharge of my duty, I tell you so. But I tell you at the same time a *fairer* duel than this I never heard of in the whole course of my life.' Needless to say, there was an immediate acquittal."

There have also been occasions where the summing-up has failed to produce the desired effect. Serjeant Adams, when acting as assistant judge at the Middlesex Sessions, was trying a case of nuisance, and in his summing-up enlarged at great

L—9

length on the definition of the offence, until the jury became both bored and tired. At length he concluded with the question, " I hope you understand the various points I have submitted to you? " " Oh yes, my Lord," said the foreman of the jury, " we are all agreed that we never knew before what a nuisance was until we heard your Lordship's summing-up."

IX

HUMOUR IN THE SENTENCE

IT is doubtful if for real wit any remark in connection with the sentence has ever equalled one made by Mr. Justice Maule. The trial was of a man accused of a serious offence, and after the jury had returned a verdict of guilty, the prisoner dramatically shouted, " May God strike me dead, my Lord, if I did it." The Judge looked grave, and paused an unusually long time before he uttered a word. At length, amid the breathless silence of the whole court, he said, " As Providence has not seen fit to interpose in your case, it now becomes my duty to pronounce upon you the lighter sentence of the Law, etc."

The language of our judges in time past partook very much of the rough nature of the times, a fact which seemed to be especially true in cases of the death sentence. Lord Eskgrove, for example, who was probably the greatest master of bathos that ever graced or disgraced the Bench, in pronouncing sentence of death, would console a prisoner by assuring him that " Whatever your religi-ous persua-shon may be, or even if, as I suppose, you be

of consolation to me that it is your verdict and not mine."

It is to Ireland, however, that we must look for the best stories of this type. At the end of the trial of a bad stabbing case at the Limerick Assizes, the usual verdict was returned, whereupon the judge addressed the prisoner as follows, " Michael, I have now to discharge you. These twelve gentlemen on my left say that you are not guilty. Take a good look at them, Mike, so that you may know them again, for if you treat any one of them the way you treated the prosecutor in this case, you will not get one hour's imprisonment from me, even if you are convicted of it."

A prisoner at the Wexford Assizes, a man of enormous physique and vicious ferocity, was indicted for highway robbery, but, largely owing to the eloquence of his counsel, the jury brought in a verdict of " Not guilty." In dismissing the prisoner, the judge, Chief Baron O'Grady, directed that he should be kept in custody until noon the following day. " May I respectfully ask your Lordship," said the astonished barrister, " why this man should have to wait until noon to-morrow? " " Because I leave Wexford at ten o'clock, and I wish to have two hours' start of your blameless client," answered the judge.

The same judge had to try a well-known virago, called Hester Carroll, for thieving. It had taken five policemen to arrest her, and as one of the witnesses passed the dock she leaned over and assaulted him savagely. There was for some time a perfect battle in court, but the Chief Baron made no comment until the woman had been reduced to harmlessness, when he quietly said, "The sentence of the court is seven years, Hester Carroll, and may God have mercy on those whose duty it will be to look after you."

Of all the stories told in connection with the unexpected verdict, there is perhaps none better than the one in which that sarcastic judge, Mr. Justice Maule, figured. The jury, to the surprise of the court, had brought in a verdict of "Guilty," and on receiving it his Lordship turned to the accused and delivered sentence as follows: "Prisoner at the Bar, your counsel thinks you innocent, I think you innocent, but a jury of your own countrymen, in the exercise of such common sense as they possess, which does not appear to be much, have found you guilty, and it remains that I should pass upon you the sentence of the Law. That sentence is that you be kept in imprisonment for one day, and as that day was yesterday, you may go about your business."

There is a good deal of humour, although much of it is of a gruesome nature, to be found in the remarks of prisoners when sentence has been passed upon them. Apropos of the fastidiousness of some offenders with regard to the judge who tries them, Lord Campbell mentions the case of a serjeant who, while acting as deputy of the Chief Justice on the Oxford circuit, asked a prisoner in the usual way if he had anything to say why sentence of death should not be passed upon him, and to his astonishment got the reply, " Only that I have been tried by a journeyman judge."

Another old criminal, with a pretty bad record, having been put back to the Quarter Sessions for trial, was sent from there to penal servitude. The fact that he had not been sentenced by what he called " a regular judge " remained one of his grievances to the end of his life. " They might have sent me up before a proper judge," he was in the habit of growling, " instead of a bloomin' amachoor."

In his earlier years at the Bar, Erskine was once retained for the defence, but so clear was the evidence that his client was soon convicted and sentenced to be hanged on the following day. As the prisoner was led from the dock, he turned to his counsel and said, " Mr. Erskine, I have not received justice." "No," replied Erskine, "that's quite true, you have not received justice. But," he added cheerfully, "you'll get it all right to-morrow."

Equally unfortunate was the prisoner who, while awaiting the decision of the jury, turned to his counsel and asked, "Do you think I shall get an honest verdict?" and received the reply, "No, for I see two men on the jury who object to hanging."

Sometimes it happens that a comment by the prisoner on his sentence may have a result that he little expected. At the Leeds Borough Sessions a man who had been sentenced to transportation for seven years shouted at the court, "I wish you may all sit there till I come back again." On this a flogging was added to his other punishment. In a second case a man convicted in a Dublin court of some trifling offence was sentenced by the judge in the following words: "The sentence of the court is that you shall be flogged from the Bank to the Quay." "Thank you, my Lord," said the prisoner, "you have done your worst." "No," returned the judge, "and back again."

X

" THE GREAT UNPAID "

THERE is probably no portion of our legal
machinery that has been so much the subject of
criticism and of good-humoured banter as the
system of voluntary magistrates—" the great unpaid "—and certainly no part that has so success-
fully withstood it. From the days of Shakespeare
the country gentleman sitting upon the Bench,
carefully shepherded by the clerk, and imbued with
the one idea that game must be preserved, has been
the butt of every wit. Nevertheless, he has come
well through the ordeal, and though it may at
times laugh at him, deep down in its heart the
British public holds the office in affectionate regard.

Shafts of wit, directed against the lack of legal
knowledge displayed by the Bench, are typified in
the story of the magistrate who, in addressing a
prisoner, said: " You say that you did not know
that you were violating the Law, but ignorance of
the Law is no excuse for any man." " Is that so? "
replied the prisoner; " well, that's rather rough on
both of us, ain't it, yer Worship? " Such taunts,
however, are in the main ill-deserved, for when a

138

magistrate has sat week by week for some years on the Bench he has at any rate a fairly good working acquaintance with the lesser kinds of crime, and is not led by the nose by the magistrate's clerk so much as is generally thought. It is somewhat surprising to find how many country magistrates have to-day a very good knowledge of the pages of that magistrates' Bible, *Stone's Justices Manual.*

An accusation that might be levied against them with more truth is that they are too prone to put aside the forms of the Law and act in accordance with their personal predilections, although this is not so frequent as it was in the olden days, when the squire ruled not only as chairman of the Bench but as the uncrowned king of the neighbourhood. In this connection a good story is told by Mr. Montague Williams of a large landed proprietor who was also the chairman of the Quarter Sessions, and who had among his labourers a very useful man who was somewhat of a favourite of his. Unfortunately, however, this man took a fancy to some of his neighbour's fowls, and being arrested and brought to trial, was sent by the local Bench to the Quarter Sessions over which his master presided. Upon the case being called the prisoner pleaded " Guilty," but the chairman went on just as if the plea had been " Not guilty." Seeing this,

the husband holding the pan while the wife turned the rashers. Being caught in the act, and having nothing to say for themselves, his Worship committed them both to jail.

Many quaint things have been said by " the great unpaid " while discharging their official duties, and in a great number of cases they have been of the nature of Irish bulls. " Are you married? " asked one magistrate of the prisoner in the box. " No, your Worship," came the reply. " That's a good job for your wife," was the sapient remark of the Bench. " Hold your tongue, and give your evidence quietly and clearly," said an Irish magistrate to a particularly voluble witness. " You're the type of man who could never look another man in his face until his back was turned," was the comment of another Irish justice.

Perhaps the best story relates to a case of an aggravated assault by a husband upon his wife, in which the latter had sustained somewhat extensive injuries. When the case came on for trial the injured woman was reluctant to give evidence, and only with difficulty could the truth be dragged from her. At last the magistrate reminded her that she must give her evidence without fear or favour, at which she cried, " Oh, I'd rather leave him to God, your Worship." " Oh dear, no," replied his Worship in a shocked tone, "it's far too serious a case for that."

Although the unpaid magistrate's idea of law may not be very well defined, it fortunately happens that his notions on equity are usually correspondingly strong. In the early days of California a rough-and-ready local magistrate held a court on Sunday, and sentenced a "greaser" (a native Mexican) to thirty-nine lashes for theft. The defending lawyer threatened to apply for a writ of *habeas corpus* on the ground that it was "unconstitootional" to hold a court on Sunday. This was too much for "his Worship," who announced with a round oath that rather than the blessed "greaser" should get off by any such pettifogging trick, he would carry out the sentence himself, which he did, remarking to the lawyer at the end of the thrashing that he had better "keep his *habeas corpus* until the 'greaser's' back got barked again." In another case, a notorious American rowdy was at last caught and brought before the magistrate. "Now, ye long, leathern, lantern-jawed Yankee cuss," said his Worship, "we've ketched you at last, and I'll commit you at once." "But," said the clerk, "you'll have to hear the evidence." "Evidence, be blowed," was the reply, "wasn't I theer, and seed it for myself?"

Sometimes in their zeal for well-doing the magistrate will give a sentence that is hardly in accordance with the Law, and it is amusing to see how his Worship will get out of the difficulty. A boy was brought before a Glasgow magistrate charged with stealing a handkerchief from a gentleman's pocket. As soon as the indictment was read, and without waiting for the evidence, the baillie, addressing the boy, said, " I hae nae doot ye did the deed, for I had a handkerchief ta'en out o' my ain pouch this verra week, so you maun gang to the jail for sixty days." At this point someone pointed out that no evidence had been taken. " Oh, in that case," replied his Worship, " I'll gie ye thirty days." On being informed that even this could not be done until guilt was proved, the worthy baillie disposed of the case by saying, " Weel, my lad, the evidence is a wee bit jumpy this time, so I'll let ye aff, but see and no' do it again."

XI

HUMOUR AMONG THE SOLICITORS

THE opinion held by the layman of the legal profession is not, generally speaking, a flattering one, and the class with which he is most often brought into contact, viz. solicitors, naturally comes in for the largest amount of criticism. " I am not prepared," said a cynic once, " to say that Brown is not honest and trustworthy, but we have to remember the fact that he is a solicitor." As further evidence of this general feeling, it may be recalled that while it is admissible for one Member of the House of Commons to call another by almost any term or epithet, and even to insinuate that he is not adhering to the strict truth, yet if he calls him a " pettifogging attorney " it has been laid down that he has exceeded the bounds of Parliamentary etiquette and must withdraw the remark at once.

If we consider the profession of solicitor as portrayed in the literary and dramatic world, it would appear that it may be divided into three classes: (1) the respectable and family, (2) the shady, and (3) the public-house solicitor, and of all three classes we have good examples in the *Pickwick*

L—10   145

Papers, where Mr. Perker represents the first, Messrs. Dodson and Fogg the second, and Mr. Pell the third. Of Mr. Perker it is unnecessary to say anything; he represents the good type of family lawyer. As regards Messrs. Dodson and Fogg, they are well described by the inimitable Sam Weller, when, in his evidence in the famous breach of promise case of Bardell *v.* Pickwick, he takes the opportunity to bring in the fact that these gentlemen " had taken up the case on spec., and were to charge nothing at all for costs unless they got 'em out of Mr. Pickwick," a benevolent attitude which they subsequently dropped. As for Mr. Pell, he speaks for himself, when in the public-house in Portugal Street he addresses Mr. Weller and his coachman friends : " Well, gentlemen, I don't wish to say anything that might appear egotistical, but I'm very glad for your sakes that you came to me; that's all. If you had gone to any low member of the profession, it's my firm conviction, and I assure you of it as a fact, that you would have found yourselves in Queer Street before this. I could have wished my noble friend (the Lord Chancellor) had been alive to have seen my management of this case. I don't say it out of pride, but I think—however, gentlemen, I won't trouble you with that. I'm generally to be found here, gentlemen, but if

I'm not here or over the way, that's my address. You'll find my terms very cheap and reasonable, and no man attends more to his clients than I do, and I hope I know a little of my profession besides. If you have an opportunity of recommending me to any of your friends, gentlemen, I shall be very much obliged to you, and so will they too when they come to know me. Your healths, gentlemen."

The two principal complaints that the general public seem to have against the so-called lower branch of the legal profession is their keenness for fees and their shifts and stratagems to obtain a verdict, and in the pursuance of these two ends it is generally considered that the profession allow their conscience to take a long holiday. As a natural sequence it would appear to follow that a lawyer cannot be honest, and if by any chance he is, then indeed he is a *rara avis*. To illustrate this common fallacy, there is the story of a solicitor who bought a ticket at a railway booking-office, found that the booking-clerk had given him a shilling too much in his change, and at once handed it back. For a moment or two the clerk stood speechless, and then, after a searching look at the lawyer, said in an awe-struck voice, " And a lawyer, too."

Much humour, too, surrounds the mystic figures " six and eight." At a dinner given to an Irish athletic team, the speaker, responding to the toast of the Irishmen, said that such sporting contests brought the two countries closer together and helped to bridge over the sixty-four miles that separated Britain from Ireland. " Pardon me," interrupted a solicitor who was present, " isn't it sixty-eight miles? " To this the speaker at once replied, " Gentlemen, don't heed this untimely interruption. My friend is a lawyer, and cannot get away from the eternal six and eight."

How far the costs in any legal transaction may be necessary is always more or less a matter of conjecture, but in many cases they appear to be out of all proportion to the amount involved. A workman had sued his employers for injuries sustained in the course of his employment, and after some litigation he had received the sum of thirty pounds. Calling upon his solicitor with the idea of settling up, he found that his bill of costs amounted to twenty pounds. With a rueful look at the ten pounds left in his hand, the workman said, " I wonder who fell off that scaffolding, you or me? "

A client, having in his pocket a five-pound note, which he thought would be more than sufficient to cover his indebtedness, called on his solicitor in order to square up. " How much do I owe you? "

he asked. "Well," said the man of law, "seeing that your father and I were old friends, we'll say fifty pounds." "Fifty pounds!" gasped the client when he recovered from the blow; "thank Heavens you didn't know my grandfather as well."

How deeply the idea is ingrained in the public mind that, no matter how large or how little the amount to be administered, it sooner or later will be dispersed in legal fees, is shown in the following story. A client who was ill sent for his solicitor to express his wishes about the disposal of his property. "That's all right," said the solicitor reassuringly, "leave it all to me." The sick man looked at him. "I suppose I might as well," he said sorrowfully, "you'll get it, anyway."

The legal, no less than the medical, profession is very much the prey of the type of individual who is always on the look-out to get something for nothing. In this connection a story is told of a close-fisted business man who, wanting advice on a knotty point of commercial law, invited a solicitor to dinner, and in the course of the meal elicited the opinion he required. On his return home, however, the lawyer, feeling that he had been done, sent in a bill for advice given. To this the merchant retaliated with a bill for dinner and wine. Not to be outdone, the solicitor reported the merchant to the Excise for selling intoxicants without a licence, and obtained the reward due from that Department to an informer.

Even if we grant that this desire to pile up fees does exist, we must have some sympathy with the young lawyer who is just entering the profession when it is considered how overcrowded it is at the present moment. To many of them it would seem that for a long time a client will be something very rare. A young solicitor was one morning putting in his time at the courts when his clerk arrived to say that a client was waiting in the office to consult him. Without a moment's delay the young lawyer started off for his office at a run. "Take it easy, sir," shouted the clerk after him, "he can't get away. I've locked him in."

The dodges to which some lawyers are said to resort in order to obtain the acquittal of a prisoner and thus enhance their own reputation reflect great credit upon their ingenuity. A man who had been accused of stealing a pig went to an American lawyer to ask him to undertake his defence. The lawyer heard the man's statement, and then asked, "Have you got the carcass?" "Yes, sir," was the reply. "Then go home," came the direction, "and cut the pig lengthwise in half and put half in my kitchen and keep the other half in yours. Don't do or say anything farther than that." When the trial came on the lawyer rose, and addressing the magistrate said, "Your honour, that man has no more of that stolen pig than I have, and if necessary I'd kiss the Bible on it." The prisoner was acquitted.

Although the solicitor, when examining a witness, stands in a favourable position, yet it sometimes happens that in the battle of wits the lawyer comes out second best, and there ensues what the reporters call "Laughter in court." The following are two typical examples.

In a case of assault a solicitor was examining one of the witnesses. "You saw that the two men were fighting," he queried, "how came it that you did not go to the help of the prosecutor?" "Well," replied the witness, "how the devil did I know which was going to be the prosecutor?"

It was the old old story of marital strife, and the husband, the accused one, was a very feeble specimen of humanity. "Do you mean to say," asked the defending lawyer, "that such a physical wreck as my client gave you that black eye?" "'E wasn't a wreck till 'e give me the black eye," said his wife triumphantly.

The rivalry that has always existed between solicitors and barristers has been responsible for many good stories. In a preceding chapter an example has been given of one where the barrister came out the victor, but in the following story the tables are turned. The witness was a solicitor, very short in stature, and he was being cross-examined by a very tall barrister. "What are you?" asked he of the wig. "I am a solicitor," was the reply. "A solicitor," laughed the barrister, who was noted for the rudeness of his examinations, "why, I could put you in my pocket." "Quite so," came the reply, "and then you would have more law in your pocket than in your head."

XII

QUIPS FROM THE COURTS

THE case was one of making and uttering counter-feit money, and the prisoner had been found guilty. "Have you anything to say in mitigation of the sentence?" asked the judge. "Yes, your Lord-ship," was the reply, "I made the money to pay for my lodgings." "Just so," quietly replied the judge, "and you made so much that it will pay for your board and lodging for the next five years."

*   *   *

Law has been described by a cynic as being like a country dance, seeing that people are led up and down in it until they are tired.

*   *   *

Addressing the court in mitigation of sentence, after his client had been found guilty, a young barrister was stopped by the judge, who said, "You are wasting the time of the court in continuing in that strain, Mr. Brief. Your client is both a knave and a fool." "Quite so, my Lord," said the bar-rister, "and he has been tried by a judge and a jury of his peers."

*   *   *

The prisoner was an Irish labourer, and the

charge that of stealing a wheelbarrow. "Have you anything to say in your defence?" asked the chairman of the Bench. "You have heard the evidence of the two witnesses, who swear that they saw you take the barrow." "Well, if it comes to that," said the prisoner, "I can find a dozen who will swear that they didn't see me take it."

       *   *   *

"Yes," said a juryman to the other eleven, "I am a plain man, and I believe in being fair to all. I don't go by what the lawyers say, and I don't go by what the judge says, but I looks well at the chap in the dock, and I sez to myself, 'That fellow must have done something, or he wouldn't be here,' so I brings 'em all in guilty."

       *   *   *

The following clever lines were once written by a barrister on a case in which he was engaged:

"He was a burglar, stout and strong,
  Who held it surely can't be wrong
  To open trunks and rifle shelves,
  For God helps those who help themselves.
"But when before the court he came,
  And boldly rose to plead the same;
  The judge replied, 'That's very true,
  You've helped yourself, now God help you!'"

       *   *   *

The jury could not come to an agreement owing to one of their number refusing to agree with the others. At length the usher was sent to ask them if they would require refreshment. " Shall I order twelve dinners? " he asked. " No," said the weary foreman, " make it eleven dinners and a bale of hay."

*   *   *

During the hearing of a case the name of the plaintiff was called, whereupon a man got up in the jury-box. " Are you the plaintiff? " said the astonished judge. " I am," replied the man. " Then what are you doing in the jury-box? " " I was chosen, my Lord, to serve on the jury." " That was a mistake, of course," said the judge; " surely you realise that a man can't sit on a jury and try his own case? " " Well," admitted the plaintiff ruefully, " I thought it was a bit of luck."

*   *   *

A lawyer defending a widow in a certain case was so carried away by his zeal that, turning to the jury, he said, " Gentlemen of the jury, a man who could be so mean as to sue a helpless widow deserves to be kicked to death by a jackass, and, gentlemen " —here he turned to the judge—" I wish his Lordship would appoint me to do the kicking."

*   *   *

" With what instrument," said the magistrate, " did your wife inflict those wounds on your head? " " With a motto, your Worship," replied the prosecutor. "With a what?" "A motto; one of them frames with 'God bless our home' in it."

*   *   *

Although much has been said about the American system of justice, it would appear that in some cases it has more sympathy with human failings than has our own. An Iowa judge recently refused to fine a man for kissing a pretty girl against her wishes, giving as a reason that "Nothing but the court's overwhelming sense of dignity prevented the court from kissing her itself."

*   *   *

Magistrate: "Do you mean to tell the court that you had only one glass of whisky?"

Prisoner (accused of drunkenness): "Only one, sorr."

Magistrate: "And where did you get that one?"

Prisoner: "Oh, at a divil of a lot of places, sorr."

*   *   *

It is generally accepted that judges make good after-dinner speakers. This is due to the fact that their sentences flow easily and with conviction.

*   *   *

The humour of the judges of the olden days was not infrequently extremely coarse. It is told of Sir Nicholas Bacon, a well-known judge of his time, that when a prisoner of the name of Hogg appealed against a sentence of death on the ground that he was related to his Lordship, the judge replied, "Nay, my friend, you and I cannot be kindred except you are hanged, for hog is not bacon until it is well hung."

*   *   *

"It would appear," said the judge, "that not only did you take all the money from the drawer, but that you also stole a quantity of valuable jewellery." "That's so, my Lord," replied the prisoner, "but you see, I was always taught that money alone does not bring happiness."

*   *   *

An old offender had been placed in the dock, and the magistrate's clerk began to read out the charge. "John Wilson, *alias* Rogers, *alias* Brown," he commenced. "Stop," said the presiding magistrate, "you haven't put Alice Rogers and Alice Brown in the dock."

*   *   *

No better example of the expression that cuts both ways has ever been given than that ascribed to Curran, the great Irish barrister. He was arguing one day before a judge, who kept shaking his head from time to time, to show that he did not agree with counsel. Curran at length turned to the jury and said, "Gentlemen, ordinary observers might imagine that the shaking of his head by his Lordship implied a difference of opinion, but you will perceive, if you remain here for many days, that when his Lordship shakes his head there's nothing in it."

*   *   *

Law in the more remote parts of our Dominions is occasionally quaintly administered. The magistrate of an up-country township in Australia was also the local storekeeper, and this is how he dealt with a " drunk " who came up before him. " It will be one pound for being drunk, five shillings for the costs of the court, and thirty-five shillings you owe me for goods supplied. Total, three pounds, or twenty-one days."

*   *   *

" I've never had a chance," complained a prisoner to his counsel; " no matter what I attempt, my unlucky number turns up." " Indeed," said the lawyer, " what is your unlucky number? " " Thirteen," came the sad reply—" one judge and twelve jurymen."

*   *   *

The present Mr. Justice Hill is said to dislike his work in the Divorce Court very much. " I have one foot in the sea and another in a sewer," he is reported to have said, referring to his dual position as a judge of the Admiralty and Divorce Divisions.

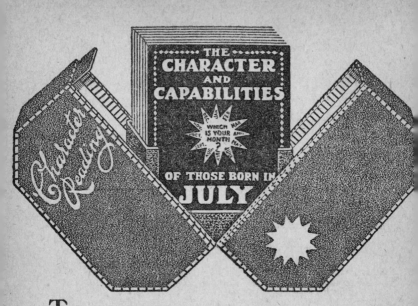

THE above is a facsimile of the most popular series of "Character Books" ever written. There are twelve of them, one for each month of the year.

CHARACTER-READING APPEALS TO ALL
THE VERY THING FOR JOLLY PARTIES

The author of these intimate Character studies is recognised as one of the leading authorities on Astrology and Phrenology, and has portrayed the Character and Capabilities of those born in each month with amazing accuracy.

This series of books is obtainable through any station bookstall or bookseller throughout the British Isles, or direct from the publishers.

Price 6*d.* each for single copies. Price for set of twelve books, including handsome case, 6*s.*

THE UNIVERSAL PRESS
CHICHESTER HOUSE, CHANCERY LANE, LONDON, W.C.2